GOING
SOLO

Hope and Healing
for the Single Mom or Dad

ROBERT BEESON

With ROBERT NOLAND

 TYNDALE HOUSE PUBLISH
CAROL STREAM, ILLINOIS

FOCUS ON THE FAMILY® | FOCUS ON PARENTING™

There simply aren't enough books with the insight and hope Robert Beeson gives in *Going Solo*. I've personally watched Robert's journey as a solo parent and have been amazed by what God has done to point him and his young girls to true north. Anyone who's been through the desert of loneliness and fear as a single parent will find encouragement and direction through Robert's story.

TROY DUHON
Executive producer, *God's Not Dead*

I love this book! Robert's journey of healing offers transformative help and hope for all solo parents who feel overwhelmed and overlooked. Let his story assure you that you are not alone.

DONNA VANLIERE
New York Times bestselling author and speaker

Beeson's debut project is honest, hopeful, and full of practical help. As he puts it, "Sometimes life doesn't turn out as we envisioned." For those struggling to make sense of being a solo parent—whether you are widowed, divorced, or separated—this book is for you.

DR. BRAD MATHIAS
Tween Gospel Alliance and Pastor of Four Winds Anglican Mission

Robert's story is humble, heartwarming, and hopeful. In *Going Solo*, he gives voice to the millions of single parents who need to know they don't have to walk alone and inspires *every* parent (including me!) to become more intentional in loving our kids well, especially when life gets crazy.

CONSTANCE RHODES
Founder and CEO, FINDING*balance*; author, *The Art of Being: Reflections on the Beauty and the Risk of Embracing Who We Are*

This book is a truly honest and transparent look at the journey of becoming a solo parent. What a great reminder of how to care for yourself and allow others to help and love you. *Going Solo* is an essential read for every individual going through loss, separation, and single parenting. All I can say is, "Wow."

PRESTON CENTUOLO
Author, speaker, and CEO of The Youth Alliance

CONTENTS

Dedicated to my daughters—Zoe, Skyler, and Zara.

My precious girls, our journey through these solo years together was the best thing to happen to me. I discovered the most fulfilling and rewarding thing in all of my life is being your father. You three brought God close to me, and I am a different man because of it. I cannot tell you how proud and honored I am to be your dad. Thanks for the patience, understanding, and strength you brought to our solo-parented family. I love you with everything in me. Always remember Isaiah 41:10.

And in memory of my late mom, Dorothy Smith, whose daily phone calls helped sustain me following my divorce.

FOREWORD

IF YOU ARE A SOLO PARENT, then you probably don't have
a lot of time to read books. But this one is worth fighting
for. It's the book I wish someone could have handed me
as I journeyed through my own season as a solo parent,
and I don't say that lightly. What Robert has written
in these pages is immediate and honest; but beyond
the openhearted stories and counsel, this book radiates
with something incredibly elusive in the season of solo
parenting—hope.

The Scriptures tell us that, "Hope deferred makes the
heart sick" (Proverbs 13:12). And if you're living a solo
parenting life right now, then you probably know how
accurate the proverb is. Hope is a much-needed companion
when life has been turned upside down and the ground
on which we stand no longer feels secure. It is the call to
take another step forward when we must provide stability
for children who have been thrust into new realities and
circumstances that are likely not of their choosing. It is a
North Star when worry and anxiety are closing in like the

hounds of hell and exhaustion is a constant companion. Hope is an irreplaceable part of the journey ahead—and hope is what *Going Solo* helps you find.

Yes, it's good to know that we are not alone on this challenging journey, but this book does more than commiserate. What you'll find as you make room for *Going Solo* in your life is safe and sacred space for your heart. It's probably been a while since you've had much of that. *Going Solo* allows you to simply listen without needing to say a word to anyone. This is a true gift. When was the last time someone poured their wisdom into you without expecting anything in return?

Going Solo wraps you in the knowledge that others have walked the road you are on and survived. It offers camaraderie in honestly approaching the singular difficulties and unique joys the solo parenting life presents. But this is far more than a memoir. Robert not only bares his soul's struggles during his season as a solo parent, he also shares practices he learned along the way that held his frayed life together—practices that can rescue what is tattered inside you.

He doesn't pander or offer lightweight solutions. Rather, he looks you in the eyes and tells you the truth:

- That this journey is going to take some time, but every step forward is worth celebrating.
- That equilibrium will return in fits and starts.
- That a new normal, which feels sane and hopeful, will happen—but not by accident.

Having lived the solo parenting story myself, I found this book to be an honest friend, a spiritual guide, and a life coach—all of which I desperately needed as a solo parent but didn't have. Thankfully, you do. You're holding that friend, guide, and coach in your hands. And if you will carve out a small space in your life for this little book, you will find it is a compass, guiding you through the murky waters of solo parenting.

As the days go by and you slowly begin to find balance once again, pass it on. There is no shortage of solo parents in the world, but there is a shortage of people willing to honestly share their story in a way that acknowledges the pain and difficulty but also falls face-first into the mercy of God—the only source of hope.

Brian Hardin
Founder, Daily Audio Bible, and author of
Sneezing Jesus: How God Redeems Our Humanity

A FEW WORDS FIRST . . .

FROM FIRSTHAND EXPERIENCE, I know the last thing you want or need as a single parent is an instruction manual to add to your already exhausting list of things to do. I get it.

Rest assured this book is *not* that. The intent of *Going Solo* is not to *fix* you. In fact, I would offer that I don't think there is anything wrong with you. I have enormous respect for the burden you are carrying and, truthfully, most people just don't realize how overwhelming your load is. I know that the single parents of the world are super-heroes in disguise.

So why do I use the term *solo* parent and not *single* parent? Because I see an important distinction between the terms. In this modern-day culture we hear about single parenting as if it's just a new normal. It is not normal. Parents were designed to parent together. It is not meant to be done alone, yet it happens. *Single* parent sounds like just another label, a box to check on forms along with your race and gender. But to me, this issue is more than a status and label. It's a condition:

Solo.
Alone.
Only.
Unaccompanied.

If you have read this far, you have felt these words and experienced the condition. *Single parent* is a status; *solo parent* is a condition.

My hope is that no matter how you got where you are—through separation, abandonment, divorce, death of a spouse, or a surprise pregnancy—that you will hear hope in my story of divorce and solo parenting. Because I've led a Solo Parent Society group that includes widows and widowers, I recognize there is a vast difference between how divorced people and widows and widowers become solo parents. Yet we still face many similar issues and emotions.

I invite you to walk with me through the many facets of the complicated solo parent life. I had to learn a lot the hard way, and I didn't do everything right, as you will see when you read my story. Because I know all too well that simply following some formula or ten-step plan will not eliminate your struggles, I simply share my story and what I've learned along the way. As you read about my challenges and hear my raw emotions, you will know you are *not* alone and that others have walked and are walking this lonely and difficult path.

I hope the examples in this book will help you, but more than that, I pray you will find, just as I did, that our heavenly Father can use this season to show Himself to you in unexpected and incredible ways. I'm praying that you will experience, maybe as never before, the eternal truth that you are loved, accepted, and cherished right where you are.

To see my personal images and videos that correspond with the events and ideas of the book I invite you to visit the *Going Solo* picture gallery exclusively available at http://soloparentsociety.com/going-solo/gallery.

1

CRAZY TIMES

I THINK I KNOW YOU. And I'll bet you know me, too. The fact that you are holding this book means there is a good chance that if you're not brokenhearted, you at least *feel* broken. Whatever circumstances led you here, the result is brokenness.

So let's be honest. No matter how you view life now, no matter how you keep score of your mistakes, and, despite people saying, "You're better off without him or her" or the opposite, "I thought you two were perfect together," well, here you are. Here we are.

If you went through a divorce as I did, you are probably feeling . . .

- alone, yet free;
- broken, yet hopeful;
- angry, yet relieved;
- sheer terror, yet strangely numb.

It's *all* in there spinning inside you—the dizzying array of emotions of feeling a freeing finality from an unbearable and seemingly hopeless situation, all the way to the absolute dread and fear of going through the rest of your life alone.

If you lost a spouse to death, I imagine the thought of finding wholeness again might even trigger a sense of guilt. You may think that moving on might be disrespectful to your late spouse, and part of you may resist returning to the wholeness you once felt.

If you are a parent who has never been married, you may feel the wonder and beauty of the life you brought into the world colliding with the fear and dread of thinking, *Who would ever want to date not just one person but a whole package?*

For all of us, it's a world of conflicting and overwhelming feelings.

If only it ended there. As if it couldn't get any worse, here's the kicker: You are now a single parent responsible for the life, welfare, care, future, and happiness of some younger souls who are facing just as much pain as you are. But they didn't get a vote in creating the mess.

The tragedy of being a single parent is that your home has been blown apart and you are now expected to be *both* parents—but, at best, you feel like *half* a parent, if that. You know you have to be strong, but you feel unable to heal your own wounds, much less piece back together the innocent hearts and souls of your children. Whether the pressure is coming from friends, family, other parents, or even your own kids, the expectations feel undeniable and daunting.

You feel deserted, kicked in the gut, and left for dead. You are going through, or have gone through, a process that points out every flaw you have for the whole world to see. Separation. Divorce. Questions. Judgments. Criticisms. Regrets. Justification. Pain. And more pain.

I know this because I have lived it. Well, survived it. And still am. Every day.

Define the Season

Right out of the gate, I want to make a few things quite clear.

Although it may feel impossible right now, you *can* get better. Healing can come. There *is* life on the other side of this. I want to share with you what I discovered in my own pain and show you that hope can be born again in your heart. Life can be fuller; relationships can be richer; you can be happier, satisfied, and content in your soul. You can journey through a transformation that, with the right perspective, will bring more good into your life and overcome all you feel you have lost. This will not be easy; it will take effort and energy. But trust me, it will be worth it. Let's face it, coming out of a marriage wasn't easy. Nothing about this is simple. Whether the divorce or loss was partly or mostly your doing (or none of your doing), or you were as surprised as anyone, there *is* hope, rest, and restoration, even in your suffering. In fact, what matters right now is what you do with *right now*.

Either the season will define you, or you will define the season.

When I decided to be intentional about how I navigated this season in my life, I discovered four principles that saved my sanity—maybe even my life. I call them my four Ps:

- Pause
- Prayer
- Practices
- Perspective

These are actually choices we make, and we will explore each one as I share my story with you. I believe God shows Himself clearly in the midst of the details of our everyday lives, and these four Ps can be threaded throughout even the mundane moments of our days.

I want to share with you what happened in my own season, not only to identify with the pain you're feeling, but also to illustrate how I walked through that time. While the details of my divorce and entry into single parenting may be quite different from yours, I'm going to bet you find yourself identifying with my feelings and relating to the pain. While I was a music industry executive at the time of my divorce, it really doesn't matter if you are a homemaker or a human resources director, a retail store clerk or a Wall Street broker. Becoming a solo parent is all about what happens within the four walls of your home and in your own heart.

My own story can be compared with a carefully constructed powder keg surrounded by people holding their fingers in their ears awaiting the explosion. Well, everyone except me.

Overnight Success

"I'm headed to the Grammy Awards," I told the unassuming, silver-haired gentleman seated next to me in first class. The flight attendant brought me my cocktail, also known as my "preflight ritual." I stirred the drink, sniffed the familiar smell of whiskey, and continued my oratory of résumé reciting.

"Yeah, I think this is the fourth year in a row my projects have been nominated, so I'm headed to LA for the awards. It's fun. I mean the show is long, the seats are uncomfortable, but there are usually one or two good acts. Truthfully, I really go for the after-parties. Those are worth the trip."

I'm not sure he was impressed, but it didn't matter—I was.

The year was 2002. It had been nine years since I'd started my company—Essential Records. Though I wasn't a musician, I was an entrepreneur who loved the entertainment industry. My record label became very successful, very quickly.

For an American missionary kid from South Africa who'd been raised in Zululand and then later attended a prep boarding school, this new life back in the States was like living in Disney World. Seemingly overnight, there were gold and platinum records. Awards. Celebrities. Traveling. Parties. Fine restaurants. Fine wine and liquor. A lot of all of it. To say I was living the high life would be an understatement.

The irony of all I just told you is my record label dealt with Christian music exclusively. Just in case you aren't familiar with this genre, this means the artists sing songs about Jesus. Here's an even stranger detail. Prior to this success in gospel music, I didn't drink alcohol, do drugs, or party. Unfortunately, the Christian music industry can be just like many other organizations run by sinners; people are involved for various reasons. I do want to make it clear, however, that there are many committed and godly people involved in this industry—there were back then and there are today. But I was widely regarded as the rebellious renegade record exec. I wasn't exactly cut from the same cloth as many of my colleagues. I took virtually every opportunity I could to "live it up."

Business and Babies

Let's rewind to 1994, when I met my wife.

While attending a music convention in my home of Nashville, Tennessee, I spotted a woman I'd met a few years earlier when I lived in California. I had not seen her since then. Strangely enough, the night before the event started I had dreamed about her. The next morning I told a friend about what happened.

"I bet she'll be here for the convention," he said. "I know she works in the industry now."

It's crazy, but she was the first person I saw at the convention. I remember thinking, *This must be a sign.* I felt as if I had been given the keys to the candy store with a pre-destined road map to pleasure. My company was quickly rising to the top, and now literally "the girl of my dreams" was standing a few feet away.

I told myself this must be God Himself handing me everything I desired. After all, I had spent most of my childhood in Africa as a missionary kid, chasing snakes and building forts with no TV, radio, or phone, cooped up in a boarding school. Now He was unleashing all at once every pleasure I had *never* had. I was making up for missing the typical American kid's life.

The "dream girl" and I reconnected that evening, and the spark was there. In my nothing-to-ninety-miles-per-hour fashion, we blew right through dating, courtship, and engagement. About three months after we met at that convention, we were married. Imagine a young woman hearing a successful record exec say, "I dreamed about you last night before I saw you here today." While true, it was also a great line to sweep a girl off her feet!

The first few years of our marriage were almost everything I hoped they would be. We lived a charmed life, traveling to Hawaii and Europe. One particular year, we enjoyed ten cruises.

The record company grew increasingly successful, and I received more and more accolades. I hired more staff. We received gold and platinum records, recognizing millions of units sold. All in all, the artists' projects I worked on were nominated for thirteen Grammy Awards, and we won five of those. We also received thirty-eight Dove Awards—the Christian music industry's equivalent to the Grammy Awards.

Money. Fame. Success. What's not to love about such a life? Depending on who you are, it can be a truly blessed journey or a road to disaster.

I can see now that during those years of managing a major record label, there were so many lessons I needed to learn. And I did learn a few of them—just not enough at the time, and not enough *in* time. Now I know that we often don't grow in maturity when life is going completely our way.

About three years into our marriage, my wife and I found out we were pregnant with our first child. We experienced the overwhelming excitement, along with the common fears, that every couple has with their first. My wife was the most beautiful pregnant woman I had ever seen, and as cliché as this might sound, she really did have a glow of grace and contentment. With new life on the way, we both believed that God was giving us a fresh start in our marriage. I knew I needed one for myself.

During those nine months, I vividly remember coming face-to-face with my shortcomings, coupled with the guilt of my transgressions, all standing in stark contrast to the beauty of new life that was about to bless both our lives.

With all the success also came the trappings and pitfalls of wealth and luxury. I had worked hard and certainly played hard. I acted as if I didn't have a care in the world, but I was always hearing the voices of guilt and shame calling out to me about what I knew were bad choices. My

behind-the-scenes partying and living it up were not consistent with the messages of hope and even godliness I had
been promoting though our label, and deep inside I knew it.
I felt like a self-absorbed counterfeit. And yet even though
I often felt like a failure before my family and God, He was
about to bless our lives, entrusting us with a child. I thought
this could bring a clean slate to our marriage and force us
to let go of our past baggage. An innocent beauty would be
relying on us, and I wanted to get this right.

I remember one night sitting upstairs in our home, listening to songs from the musical *Les Misérables*. In what
remains to be one of my favorite songs of all time, the
character of Jean Valjean sings "Bring Him Home." After
observing the beautiful love that a young man, Marius, has
for his daughter, Jean prays to God on the war-torn barri-
cade, asking Him to save Marius's life—"to let him live"—
even if it means that God must take his life instead.

The words moved me deeply, describing the depths of
my own soul. As I listened to this song repeatedly, my spirit
was singing this song to God, telling Him how I had failed
so many times yet was amazed that He would choose to
bless me anyway. I asked Him to please not hold my transgressions against my child, to "let her live," and to make
only me responsible for the wrongdoings of my life.

I was overwhelmed by the great love that I was experiencing—more love than I had ever understood before. I already
loved this child more than anything in my life, and we hadn't
even met.

Our first daughter, Zoe, was born in January 1997. As

I cut the cord, we heard her first cry. She was healthy and beautiful. We were blessed.

If you are a mother, please forgive me. I know my words pale in comparison to the intense emotions you surely know how to articulate. But as a father, I was experiencing something far deeper and grander than ever before in my life.

Remember the hope for a fresh start and the prayers of pleading and gratitude I mentioned? After experiencing the sacredness of my firstborn's birth, after facing and confessing my own personal failures and shortcomings head-on, any reasonable man would have course-corrected to a new destination. But that's not what I did.

I dove deeper than ever before into my business and industry relationships as my professional success continued. My staff became like family, and I allowed them to compete with my real family.

Over the next four years, we welcomed two more daughters, Skyler and Zara. Each of their births was a spiritual experience—profound and beautiful. Each time I felt as if I were coming up for air after being underwater in a sea of selfishness for far too long, as if God were giving me His breath.

All the while, the work of my hands was turning out rewarding and reverent songs that contributed to one of the best seasons in Christian music history. To this day, I feel privileged to have been involved in those projects and working with those artists.

One of the recordings I had the honor of developing was a worship series entitled *City on a Hill*, which remains one of my favorite musical endeavors. For the record release, we premiered the project at a legendary musical venue called the Orpheum Theater in New Orleans at the International Christian Retail Show, an annual convention.

During one of the songs, "God of Wonders," which involved various well-known artists all engaged in worship, I remember being so moved and humbled that I went downstairs underneath the stage and wept through the entire song. As I cried, the words and melody moved through the venue's speakers and into my spirit. I was witnessing the beautiful things that God was creating and blessing me with yet pursuing my own self-centered and narcissistic desires. So often, the Father moves and works His will in spite of us.

Unveiling to you the constant thread of God pursuing my heart is crucial to where we take this subject matter. I'm telling you that I was living my life as if it were all about me to help us all understand that life is not about us!

Monetizing Manure

Do you remember when I was bragging about my accomplishments to the guy in first class on my way to the Grammys? Just after takeoff, somewhere around my second drink and after reciting all my accomplishments and successes to this captive audience seated beside me, I decided to take a break and ask him what he did for a living. You know, just to not seem too self-focused.

His answer: "I'm in manure sales."

Wow, I thought. *This guy sells poop*! My view of my

career immediately went up a few notches. Manure sales had to be one of the most laughable jobs I had ever heard of. But this guy was sitting in first class, next to me. That means there had to be at least some money in, uh, poop.

On the heels of that comment, I thought it would be nice to take control of the conversation again. So I fired off that my company had gained about $80 million in revenue the previous year. Without missing a beat and emitting a humble elegance, this man delivered a massive gut-punch of perspective with his response: "Last year, my territory did around half a billion dollars in sales."

I quickly compared his half a billion to my $80 million. He won—I wasn't even close!

No one hands out awards in LA, or anywhere else for that matter, for monetizing manure. No one would think the payout on poop is sexy. But with one sentence, this unassuming guy deflated every sail on my boat. He reminded me of a vital concept that I desperately needed to learn. Perspective is important. There's always someone bigger, faster, and smarter, whether it's your neighbor or your competitor. Things are often not actually as they seem. I know my life certainly wasn't.

Giving Up Control

During the tenth year of our marriage, my wife and I were in regular counseling and I had started to clean up my act. The change came after three dramatic things happened within a six-month period.

First, I found out we were pregnant with our third daughter on the same day as the September 11 attacks.

Second, during an afternoon soccer game, one of my far-too-young friends "fell wrong" on the field and died a few days later.

Third, and probably the most profound, my friend and I got drunk one night at an impromptu company party and vandalized a promotional vehicle owned by an artist known as TobyMac. Toby is a veteran Christian singer/songwriter who was also a friend and colleague. The incident was captured on video, and this was before *everything* was caught on camera. In our inebriated state, we had convinced each other that everyone would think this was just a funny gag, a practical joke. Needless to say, that wasn't everyone's perspective. (More on this story later.)

These situations taught me one thing: No matter how much we might think we have life under control, we don't. In reality, there's only a thin thread of grace separating our demise from our finest hour. Whether by an act of our own hand, a terrorist attack, or a freak accident at a soccer game, life can end—or change dramatically—in a moment. The life we wake up to on any given day is a gift.

In marriage counseling, my wife and I directed a fair amount of blame at each other for various reasons, some legitimate and some not. Sometimes the storms of life do irreversible damage. In fact, they can so devastate that there's nothing visibly left intact. My spiritual paradigm certainly allows for the fact that God can do anything, but in a marriage both have to cooperate and allow Him to work to accomplish what *He* wants.

Career, success, money, kids, marriage, or even just the busyness of life can keep us believing we are making forward progress. But if we start making the activities and our ambitions the source of our security, in what seems like only a second our lives can be forever altered, taken from us, or at the very least, our deep emptiness can be exposed.

Back in those days, I latched on to *anything* that created the appearance of progress. I was blind to the fact that I had become caught up in the *perception* of forward motion. In truth, I was standing still, and our marriage was headed directly into a devastating storm made by our own hands.

Even though I had built such a poor foundation for my family, when my wife finally left the girls and me, I couldn't remember how we had gotten to this place. And in that moment of realization, it really didn't matter. All I knew was this: What once was, now wasn't. And it seemed as if it happened in a heartbeat.

SOLO CONFESSIONAL

"I felt horrific shame and embarrassment as a parent, a man, and a Christian. I tried to hold on for as long as I could even during all my wife's affairs. Long after the fact, I began recalling all the red flags and felt that I had made a big mistake. Somehow my ego told me that I could be bigger than the problem and that my love was all it would take to fill the holes in her heart. I repented, and still do, daily for the sins of not totally seeking God first and for ignoring the signs. When she asked for a divorce, I refused to file, hoping that I could eventually turn things around. I didn't want anyone to know, perhaps to avoid the finality of it all, perhaps out of embarrassment. I felt that my witness as a Christian was irreparably damaged."

JIM

The Rain Sender

Sometimes life doesn't turn out as we envisioned. Consider what happened one Saturday morning in my neighborhood as I opened my windows to let in the springtime breeze. The birds were chirping, and I could hear my neighbors tackling their weekend chores of washing the car and mowing the lawn. I had just shut my eyes to take a brief nap when I was startled awake by someone screaming. This was not a playful outburst.

I jumped up, ran to my front door, and looked outside to see a teenager lying on the ground, screaming in agony. Our neighbor's son, an all-star high school football player, had lost his footing on the slick grass while mowing. As he fell, his right foot slid under the mower into the powerful blades. I quickly saw that this was a significant injury and potentially the finish to his career, the sudden end of his hopes and dreams.

His headphones were dangling by his side, still playing the music he was listening to only five minutes before when he was in a very different state of mind. The contrast is stark: One minute it's a beautiful spring day and you're enjoying some tunes while mowing the lawn. Then the next minute comes—and tragedy strikes.

The fact that life can change so suddenly is crazy to me. No one is immune. No one is safe. There are no guarantees that we will not experience pain and suffering in our lives, at times unforeseen and completely undeserved.

When my wife left, you could say I had it coming, considering the way I was living. The truth is that I did sow a great deal of destruction.

But you couldn't say that about my neighbor's son. He had nothing coming to him except good. What did he do for this to happen? Nothing. He ended up losing two of his toes, which set him back in his football career. But he fought on to rehabilitate and even earn a university scholarship. Just as that young man was injured, many spouses and children are cut deep by divorce. They didn't see it coming, and they don't deserve it either. Yet it happens— shattering hopes, dreams, hearts, and lives.

Because of life's volatility I have a long-standing love/ hate relationship with Matthew 5:45: "He causes his sun to rise on the evil and the good, and sends rain on the righteous and the unrighteous." Unexpected and seemingly undeserved hardships don't seem fair and can cause us to blame someone or something, even if there really isn't anyone or anything to blame.

But what if it's completely clear who or what caused the damage? Blame won't change the brokenness. Pointing fingers can't and won't bring healing. In fact, doing so only infects the soul.

Blame, bitterness, unforgiveness, hatred, and even revenge will not bring comfort or healing or satisfaction. These deflective distractions only deepen the pit we can fall into. We feel broken. We feel alone. We feel abandoned and betrayed.

I knew that no matter how I ended up in that moment of divorce and solo parenting, I was most certainly *there*. And so were my soon-to-be ex-wife and my three innocent daughters.

And it's the same for you: No matter how it happened, you are here in this solo parent situation, with your fears, failures, disappointments, anger, exhaustion, questions, chaos, and brokenness.

The Game Changer

Undoubtedly, 2006 was the hardest year of my entire life. I was burned out in my personal life and my career. It was the year I chose not to renew my contract as head of artist development with Provident Label Group—a Christian music conglomerate. It was also the year my marriage ended.

For the sake of my girls and their mom, I am going to leave out the details of my ex's behaviors that led to her leaving and the court's ultimate ruling giving me full custody of my three girls and supervised visitation with their mom. Although she filed for the divorce and left the girls and me, I had legitimate legal and biblical grounds for ending the marriage. In our situation, I agreed that divorce was in the best interest of everyone, most importantly the girls.

So regardless of how we got where we are, how do we

begin to put the pieces back together? That's a tough question to ask when the best we can hope for is surviving today while trying not to lose any more than we have already lost.

So the question must go deeper than "How?" and certainly get past "Why?"—although it's easy to constantly ask ourselves both of those questions.

For me, the questions became "Who?" and "Where?"

Who am I now that the bottom has dropped out of my life?

Who am I now that everything is stripped bare?

Where am I? Where do I belong? Where do I go from here? Where *can* I go from here?

Even though I was still breathing and God had given me the grace of another day, there were many mornings that I just did not *want* a new day. I only wanted the nightmare to end. The grace of a new dawn brought me no comfort. But my questions of "Who?" and "Where?" began to be answered from an odd source.

Early in 2007, I scheduled a meeting over coffee with the man who originally bought my company and moved me from LA to Nashville. At this point in my career, I was trying to start a new business, and he would be taking care of manufacturing and distributing the product to retail.

I needed a $20,000 advance to finish a recording. Now, depending on your reference, that may sound like a lot of money, but during that time in the music industry, it was actually a modest request with the potential of a quick return. Due to my track record in the industry, I expected this would be a no-brainer. And this particular man had always been fond of my entrepreneurial spirit.

He listened as I told him how my wife had left, how I was raising three girls on my own, and starting this new business. After he tuned in intently, he politely and quite casually said, "No, Robert." In fact, he said the words as if he were doing me some kind of favor.

To my surprise, he then added, "But I do want to buy you a book." Although my face remained expressionless, inside I was screaming, *Are you kidding me?! I ask for a business loan and you offer to buy me a book?!*

But this guy had a knack for doing things his own way. The coffee shop was in a bookstore, so I followed him over to a section where he perused the titles and pulled out his gift to me. As he handed me the book, he said, "Now, don't tell anyone I'm buying you this, because a lot of people might view this message as 'new age.'" My friend was a very conservative Christian. Still somewhat offended that he would have the audacity to *not* grant my request for money, I assured him this exchange would stay between us.

Well, as you might suspect, my friend had given me just what I needed. I just couldn't see it in that me-focused moment.

Since God can use anything He wants when He wants, I heeded the book's message to zero in on what I came to call the *constant*. This simple concept saved my life. My prayer, as we move forward together, is that it can save yours, too. I do want you to know as you press on in this book that you are not alone, so please start thinking "we" more than "me."

This level of inward-focused hard work must be intentional, so let's get started.

2

VOICE OF TRUTH

DURING THE LAST month of my marriage, I had moved into an upstairs bedroom. On one beautiful spring morning, I came down the stairs to sense an eerie stillness. Then I noticed the open door that was always closed up tight this time of day. Suddenly, there was no air to breathe. The silence was screaming. My mind was racing.

That open door led to our master bedroom.

She was gone.

Not left-for-work or headed-to-the-store or I'll-be-back-later gone, but gone for good.

Somehow, I just knew it. I could feel *it*.

There had been times in the past when I had felt that "I just know" feeling. I had suspected this moment at other points in our marriage. But this time, it was real—as in-your-face real as anything I had ever experienced before.

All the lists of evidence, all the stories I had shared with friends, all the suspicions I had carried around were so completely insignificant compared with the gravity and certainty of this moment.

I didn't have to check the bedroom or even call her name. This was different. My pastor aptly calls these moments "the presence of absence." It's like the shell of a body in the casket when a soul has left. Here I was, viewing a death.

I knew I only had a matter of minutes before the girls would come bolting down the stairs asking about Mommy. This time I knew I couldn't bluff my way through a story. I didn't have a reason or a ray of hope to share anymore. They needed to know.

The Condition

The pattern we had created during the previous few years of our marriage had been chaotic and exhausting. Here's the truth—I was completely done in from it all.

After my wife left, I found myself in a brand-new place, in a circumstance you wouldn't wish on anyone. I was shocked by my family's new normal. You never realize the sounds of companionship until they're gone and all you are left with is an incredibly noisy hush. What I did hear were the thoughts of shame, fear, regret, and confusion that filled my mind.

My friends were supportive for the most part, but I couldn't help but feel an undertow of a few thinking,

Of course this happened! Why do you sound so surprised?
I wasn't surprised; I just didn't want to believe it had really
happened.

We have sayings in our culture like "When it happens,
you will know it's right" and "If it is meant to be, it will
be." When *it*—the situation—arrives, it's undeniable. This
it is what I call the *condition*.

The Constant

For me, the key to handling those first stages of this
great abyss without completely losing my mind was actually quite simple. But it's so easily and often overlooked.
The key was, and still is, being aware of what I deem the
constant.

Being aware of the *constant* requires taking a full
account of what your reality *actually* is, not what it *appears*
to be. You will need to function as an observer of the situation, instead of being defined by the situation.

I believe this is part of what Jesus is talking about in
Matthew 6:25-33.

> Therefore I tell you, do not worry about your life,
> what you will eat or drink; or about your body, what
> you will wear. Is not life more than food, and the
> body more than clothes? Look at the birds of the air;
> they do not sow or reap or store away in barns, and
> yet your heavenly Father feeds them. Are you not
> much more valuable than they? Can any one of you
> by worrying add a single hour to your life?

And why do you worry about clothes? See how the flowers of the field grow. They do not labor or spin. Yet I tell you that not even Solomon in all his splendor was dressed like one of these. If that is how God clothes the grass of the field, which is here today and tomorrow is thrown into the fire, will he not much more clothe you—you of little faith? So do not worry, saying, "What shall we eat?" or "What shall we drink?" or "What shall we wear?" For the pagans run after all these things, and your heavenly Father knows that you need them. But seek first his kingdom and his righteousness, and all these things will be given to you as well.

I love the fact that Jesus not only reminds us about His care for us, but that He also asks us to change our focus in practical ways to respond to that care. Jesus tells us not to worry because He sees the big picture. No matter what *condition* we face, that circumstance is not the whole story or the big picture. There is a much larger context and reality—the *constant*—that exists beyond what's right in front of us.

The *constant* is accurate and trustworthy, while the *condition* is just a piece of the story and always provisional. The *constant* is permanent; the *condition* is temporary.

Taking a snapshot of a mountain cannot adequately capture the scope and majesty of the beauty surrounding it. In the same way, our current condition cannot possibly represent our entire reality.

Yet God always knows our entire reality. He offers us the constant: His truth and viewpoint. He is never sur-

prised or caught off guard, even when the world seems
to have turned upside down and landed on you. Jesus
ends this teaching with a profound closer: "Therefore
do not worry about tomorrow, for tomorrow will worry
about itself. Each day has enough trouble of its own"
(Matthew 6:34).

Let's be honest—the *condition* is often a lie. It's the tale
we tell ourselves. It's the story the enemy tells us. Remember
those movie scenes when the hero is being chased and runs
into a dead-end wall? We have no idea how he'll escape.
Then the camera angle changes and we see the circumstance
differently: There's a hidden lever or some other apparatus
to provide safe passage. That's how I grew to see my *condition*. My wall, my dead end, just like yours, is seldom what
it seems to be. If we change our perspective, we'll see a new
path right in front of us. Yes, the giant barrier is actually
there, but so is the way out. The *condition* does not define
or trap us.

The situation in which we find ourselves during
these dark hours can be navigated only with the correct
perspective—the *constant*, the viewpoint of God.

In my first few months of being a solo parent, I would
go into my room, close the door, lie down flat on the floor,
and find the stillness, reminding myself of the truth:

"God is *completely* in control."

"This has *not* caught Him off guard."

"He intimately *loves* me and my kids."

"He is big enough to create the universe, so He will
carry us through this."

"I must simply look to *Him*."

My job was, and still is, to trust *Him*—not the way
things appeared, how I felt, the whispers in my head, or
even the well-meaning voices around me. I needed to
trust Him *in the moment* and not worry about the next.
I needed to put one foot in front of the other, even if I
was crawling.

I understand that right now hanging on to the truth
may feel impossible to you; you might feel as if that giant
wall is blocking your way. But believe me, choosing this
much-needed mind-set and using the practical exercise I
describe later in this chapter are the best choices you can
make for your family's survival.

Feelings Versus Facts

Working to quiet my mind was probably the most difficult battle I faced, while ironically also being the most
significant life preserver in those early days of being solo.
This brings us to the first of the four Ps I introduced
earlier:

Pause.

I had never craved quiet time all alone more than I did
in that season. I had never been so insistent on finding
even fifteen minutes of solitude before the Lord. I needed
to be still and know and confess that He is God, that He is
the constant in my life.

There is a huge difference between *the condition* and *the
constant*, just as there is a huge difference between feelings
and facts.

One of the records I had the privilege of working on

was by a then-unknown band of youth workers from Georgia named Casting Crowns. The lead singer, Mark Hall, has an amazing testimony of working to overcome severe dyslexia that plagues him to this day. Each time he walks onto a stage and opens his mouth to sing and speak, he faces the decision of which voice he will listen to—his condition or his Counselor, his *condition* or God's *constant*. The lyrics of "Voice of Truth" by Mark Hall and Steven Curtis Chapman propelled me to make the leap from my own condition to the truth of my Counselor, to trade my *condition* for God's *constant*.

> *But the waves are calling out my name and they*
> *laugh at me*
> *Reminding me of all the times I've tried before and failed*
> *The waves they keep on telling me time and time again,*
> *"Boy, you'll never win!"*
> *"You'll never win!"*
> *But the voice of truth tells me a different story*
> *The voice of truth says, "Do not be afraid!"*
> *The voice of truth says, "This is for My glory"*
> *Out of all the voices calling out to me*
> *I will choose to listen and believe the voice of truth.*[1]

After the crash of losing a spouse occurs and we are pulled from the wreckage, we find ourselves exhausted from "keeping all the plates in the air"—juggling the kids, lawyers, bills, and job as we wrestle with our sanity and worry about what everyone is going to say. The voices in our head can be so loud:

You failed.
You're not enough.
There's no hope.
You can't do it.
You are all alone.
Everything is lost.
You're not worth fighting for.
You will never be loved again.

When those thoughts start becoming beliefs, we need to "choose to listen and believe the voice of truth." Only when we make time to do this can we understand and embrace the realization that we are held gently and tenderly, yet firmly, in the hands of the One who loves us more than anything on Earth. From experience, I want to assure you that God alone is able to carry you through this season. Even if you don't feel God's presence right now, He is with you.

One of my friends in our local Solo Parent Society group, Kevin, told me about the days just after he lost his wife to a brain tumor, which left him a *solo* dad raising three young girls. "I really wasn't mad at God, but I did want to understand 'Why?' That led me to question His goodness and His intentions. At some point, I knew that I was not actually living out the truths that I had believed most of my life. I either needed to change the way I was thinking or change what I believed to make the two compatible. So I chose to change my thinking. Each morning when I woke up, and then throughout the day, I would pray, 'Father, I love You. I trust You and know You are good. I want what You want.' Early on, I usually added, 'I really don't feel this way but I want to feel this way.' It took a couple of months, but eventually, those statements moved from my head into my heart, and I really did mean what I was saying."

This conversation reminded me of the story in Exodus when the Israelites were terrified as the Egyptian army was quickly approaching and they were backed up against the Red Sea, seemingly about to meet their demise. I am certain the voices in their heads were screaming *This is it!* as they sarcastically complained to Moses, "Have you brought us out here to die in the desert because there were not enough graves for us in Egypt?" (Exodus 14:11, TLB). But I love the truth Moses delivers to the terrified nation completely overwhelmed by their condition: "Do not be afraid! Stand firm and you will see the deliverance the LORD will bring you today. The Egyptians you see today you will never see again. The LORD will fight for you; you need only to be still!" (Exodus 14:13-14).

The voice of truth says, "Don't be afraid. Be still. The Lord is fighting for you."

I have always *believed* that God fights for me, but in the midst of a crisis I don't necessarily *feel* that way. Like Kevin said, either we believe what we say or we have to change what we believe.

The *condition* is circumstantial, situational, and based on what is happening to you and what you see and feel.

The *constant* reminds us to recognize our condition in context of the never-changing reality of our heavenly Father's love, care, and power to change anything—and everything.

The condition constantly changes. The constant never does and never will. This truth reminds us of Hebrews 13:8: "Jesus Christ is the same yesterday and today and forever."

When God appeared to Moses in the burning bush and told him to rescue the Israelites from Egypt, He also told Moses his name.

> Moses said to God, "Suppose I go to the Israelites and say to them, 'The God of your fathers has sent me to you,' and they ask me, 'What is his name?' Then what shall I tell them?" God said to Moses, "I AM WHO I AM. This is what you are to say to the Israelites: 'I AM has sent me to you.'"
>
> EXODUS 3:13-14

And when Jesus spoke to the Pharisees, He made His name and identity clear.

> "Very truly I tell you," Jesus answered, "Before Abraham was born, I am!"
>
> JOHN 8:58

I love the way noted theologian Albert Barnes describes I AM: "The words express absolute, and therefore unchanging and eternal Being."[2]

To me, there is no better way to explain the idea of the constant than to embrace the absolute, unchanging, and eternal existence of I AM in the midst of our condition.

Regardless of who's to blame in your situation, the reality of your life in God's *constant* presence is safe and intact. Although you may feel very alone—you are not.

God loves you constantly.

He holds you constantly.

He cares deeply about what you and your kids are going through in your condition.

Embracing the constant of our God, the I AM, is where He will meet you, as you are, no matter how messy life may be. And as He told us, "Tomorrow will bring its own worries. Today's trouble is enough," (Matthew 6:34, NLT).

Rest in the Constant

Let's talk about how to put this chapter into practice. After all, if there is no application for change, what good is this discussion to your life? Consider this verse from Matthew:

> Here's what I want you to do: Find a quiet, secluded place so you won't be tempted to role-play before God. Just be there as simply and honestly as you can manage. The focus will shift from you to God, and you will begin to sense his grace.
>
> MATTHEW 6:6, MSG

I want you to take five minutes to be still before God. At first, this may seem awkward, but we are going to do what the verse says: Find a comfortable and quiet spot. Shut the door. Put your phone on silent. Close your eyes. Breathe deep and slow—in through your nose, out through your mouth. Repeat. Just listen to your breathing.

Think of all the life you are taking in—the clean, refreshing oxygen filling your lungs. Whatever you are facing today, God is with you whether you feel His presence or not. He is very real and very present in your *condition.*

Try these words: "Father, I surrender to You. Please help me." Repeat.

Give up all your struggles, burdens, and worries to the One who is sustaining you. After all, up to this moment, you may not have noticed that God has been holding you and sustaining you all along, just as you aren't aware of your breathing. The God who created all things, knows all, is in control of all, is with you. He is fully aware of what is going on in your life—uncontrollable kids, angry ex, unpaid bills, lack of time, distancing friends—everything. He is able to keep you going, and you can trust Him in this quiet place.

This is the *constant.*

Rest and *know* He is God.

3

I NEED A MIRACLE

I REMEMBER THE FIRST TIME I saw the Christian group Casting Crowns in concert. They were playing in Orlando for a showcase at a Christian retailers convention. I was asked to assist them since this would be their first time performing in front of Christian industry leaders.

When I saw how many people were in the group I remember thinking, *There is no way this will ever work.* In my "expert" opinion, there were simply too many people on stage. With creativity, egos, and all I knew about how bands work—and don't work—I didn't think these folks could make it. I was wrong. Why? Unity through servant-leadership made them one of the most cohesive bands I have ever witnessed. Our first record together sold two million copies. Obviously, I was completely fine with being wrong on this one.

But I still often asked myself why Mark Hall, the founder and leader, didn't choose to be a solo act. After all, he was the songwriter, lead singer, and spokesperson for the band. Over time, I saw Casting Crowns's biblical power of strength in numbers. Mark understood that truth well. When people surrender to a common cause, the impact can change the world—especially when the purpose is ordained by God. The power of experiencing harmony, both in music and in calling, is much greater together. I believe they call that synergy—the idea that the whole is greater than the sum of its parts.

In the same way, a marriage that is unified and led effectively is a powerful force. But in either case, this doesn't come easily. Constant surrender, grace, and respect, to name just a few qualities, must be continually practiced and deepened.

Jesus Christ, while being the only Son of God, chose to travel in a group. He led the most successful and influential band of all time because they started the church we all still attend today! God Himself saw the value in not traveling alone. After all, He is a Community—Father, Son, and Holy Spirit. Each of His disciples brought his own characteristics to the overall picture, and God used this unique mixture of mankind to change the course of history.

But when Jesus needed to recharge spiritually, mentally, and emotionally, He didn't say, "All right guys, we've worked hard, feeding thousands, healing the sick, and raising the dead. We deserve a break, so let's all pack it up and head to our favorite resort on the Mediterranean for an all-inclusive package!"

No. When Jesus needed strength, He pulled away from the band and went solo for a bit. In the desert, on the other side of the Sea of Galilee, and even in His darkest hour in Gethsemane, He left the community and alone sought His most important relationship—the one with His Father. As a Christian, *solo* never really means alone.

We often find our strength in numbers just as Casting Crowns does, so that collectively, as in the body of Christ, God can use us to change the world.

But even if you don't feel you are part of the body right now—or part of anything—be assured that God has specifically designed plans for you. God sees you as the unique person He created; He knows the "big picture" and sees your purpose as an individual.

God's big-picture plans for us as individuals remind me of my former boss, Clive Calder. After he signed the supergroup boy band *NSYNC to the mainstream side of our label, Clive told me in his distinct South African accent, "Yeah, the group will do well, but the real secret is the young man, Justin Timberlake. I expect his solo career to eclipse what the group does." As we all know, Clive saw the "big picture" for Justin Timberlake.

Remember, God sees your "big picture." His purpose for you may involve community, but His interest and passion for you is exclusive,

personal,

singular,

solo.

Spend solo time with your Father, just as Jesus did, so you can gain strength and direction for your new life, the life God has planned for you.

Solo Season

There will be times, whether of our own doing or not, that we are pushed into being solo. The story of Joseph in the book of Genesis is an extreme example of this dynamic. The young man lived in a loving home as the favorite of a doting father, but because of his brothers' horrible jealousy, he was forced out, sold into slavery, left abandoned and alone!

At that time of crisis and abandonment, Joseph didn't know his outcome. But God was writing the young man's story; He knew Joseph would be apart from his family for a long time. He would be alone and, as a result, would eventually save his family and also impact world history.

The pattern continued repeatedly, with Joseph being singled out by Potiphar's wife, prisoners, guards, and even the king. For many reasons, he was forced to go solo, but he eventually rose to be the most powerful person in the world, next to the king himself.

Even if we agree that God has a plan for us, just as He did for Joseph, there is still something unnerving and ominous about the deafening silence of being alone. Especially when it feels sudden.

At the time I felt most alone, I was actually not alone at all. Remember when I walked downstairs, found the open bedroom door, and knew my wife was gone for good?

Right after that moment, my three beautiful daughters

walked into the kitchen where I was. They began to ask where Mommy was that morning. Nothing had ever weighed so heavy on my shoulders as those few questions and minutes did. I couldn't lie and tell them that everything was going to be okay, that Mommy was coming home soon. I had to be honest, and I knew it would hurt them.

That crisis of decision took me back to the moment when my own mom delivered the news of my parents' divorce. I remember the questions that flooded my sixteen-year-old mind that day.

- What does this mean?
- What's going to happen?
- Where will I live?
- What will this look like?
- Will I ever see my dad again?
- Will my mom ever be the same?
- Will I still be loved?
- Are we still a family?
- Does what I think matter?
- Do *I* matter?

A tsunami of emotions rushed over my heart. And I was now unleashing that exact same storm on my own daughters.

For a few fleeting seconds, I actually thought of ways I could spin the story, fix this, lessen the blow, or completely avoid this crushing crossroads. But then I had a mental collapse. I realized I was exhausted to the bone. So I surrendered to the truth—so help me, God.

"Girls," I started, "you know Mommy and I have been

having some really hard times. It breaks my heart because I know you have seen a lot. Well, this morning when I got up, I realized your mom had left. I'm fairly sure she is safe, but I really don't know when she is coming back. I am so sorry that I have to tell you this because I know how hard this is to hear. I want you to know that I am here, I will never leave you, and although I imagine things are going to be tough on us for a while, I know we will get through this together."

I gathered them all up, pressing each one into my chest. And I held them. I held them in such a way as to send a permanent message to each one of their little hearts that this hug was going to last forever—no matter what. Many big tears were shed. But, strangely, I could literally feel the truth setting us free, the weight of hiding being lifted from all four of us. We *were* in this together, and even though an aching pain came that day that would never fully leave, I could tell that our heavenly Father was there in our "valley of the shadow of death." He doesn't promise that we will never be in that valley, but He most certainly is faithful to His promise to be there with us.

Some of the sweetest memories I have in my life are from that early season of just crawling to get through each day. Even though being a single parent can feel over-whelming, the dark times I went through with my girls became the most precious moments of my life: the four-day vacations to Rosemary Beach, the nights at home when we would sit on the floor with four spoons and a gallon of chocolate ice cream between us, our times of earnest daily prayer together when we asked and believed God would provide. There is something about being authentically broken that creates deep bonds—and those bonds remain well beyond the end of difficult circumstances.

When I was in the chaos of the day-to-day, I rarely found the appropriate perspective. But whether I chose to sequester myself away or didn't have a choice and was left all alone, without fail, God provided moments of peace and reassurance, even on the most difficult days. Right after the divorce, when the girls would stay with their grandmother who lived fifteen minutes away, I rarely made plans to do anything. Instead, I would come back to a quiet house, which was usually filled with the sounds of energetic little girls, make myself dinner, and sit alone in the quiet and eat. Strangely enough, I rarely felt alone. When things were still, I felt a quiet companionship. I sensed His presence. When I surrendered the illusion that I was in control, my spirit rested.

Perhaps God can use your *solo* season in this same way, even through the pain and confusion. He alone knows the outcome of your story, and He's writing it for you right now, just as He did with Joseph.

> Because the patriarchs were jealous of Joseph, they sold him as a slave into Egypt. But God was with him and rescued him from all his troubles. He gave Joseph wisdom and enabled him to gain the goodwill of Pharaoh king of Egypt. So Pharaoh made him ruler over Egypt and all his palace.
>
> ACTS 7:9-10

God can use *solo* seasons to make us stronger and create a new path. These times alone with Him are meant for building intimacy and trust—even if we cannot see His purpose in the moment.

While marriage and community are awesome, God wants to have an intimate relationship with you—and that one-on-one relationship is not reliant on your spouse, church, or peer group.

We were created to be in a relationship with God. He loves harmony and people coming together—doing life in a group—but your strength and fulfillment will only come when you approach Him alone, just as Jesus did. In that moment, it's not about your marriage, divorce, remarriage, kids, or job. It's about a relationship specifically tailored to you.

I truly don't believe I ever experienced the depth of how much God loved me until after my divorce. Don't get me wrong: I would never have chosen that to be the way God revealed His love for me. But knowing what I know now, I am not at all sure I would understand the concept of my Father's intense love and provision had it not been for that season.

I had always approached the world through the individual lenses of my many roles—husband, father, friend, businessman, creative, and so on. But God says I am whole and *all* His. Regardless of how many platinum records I sold, how many Grammys I won, or how many narcissistic pursuits that led me to fail at being a fully engaged husband and father, I am His. He doesn't look at our qualifications, titles, roles we play, or affiliations. He made me for Him. He made you for Him. We are made perfect and able to enter community only after we embrace who we are in Him. And the only way to Him is solo, not through a group. He calls us out of where we are and how we view ourselves to know Him. And in this relationship we begin to know ourselves as a reflection of His image.

Somehow along the way in life, we fool ourselves into thinking we are defined by the life we choose, rather than the One who created us, chose us, called us, and said we are enough because of Him.

Being forced into a solo season is the perfect time to embrace or deepen the way God intended us to experience Him.

The Bridge to Healing

My mom, a licensed counselor and therapist, was a godsend throughout our entire divorce. One day she told me, "Robert, don't overlook the anger. It's normal. You need to let it out. Vent. I suggest you take a few things that represent your marriage and, in the right setting, destroy them—break them, burn them, shred them. Attach the significance of your relationship to those items and 'ceremonially' destroy them." So I listened to my mom's wisdom and did just that.

One of the meetings my ex-wife and I went through was mediation. In case you aren't familiar with this concept, it's where a neutral party sits with you and your spouse and tries to reach an agreement as to how the divorce should be transacted. On this particular occasion, we actually reached an agreement. This moment was half heartbreak, half relief. Afterward, I went home and gathered things that symbolized our marriage—plates we had bought together in Italy, a bronze plaque, framed pictures, Valentine's Day and anniversary cards, along with various other mementos. I also grabbed a large pillowcase.

On my way out the door to the garage, I walked by our crystal glass display case. I had always cherished and collected these fine glass pieces, particularly the heavy Baccarat crystal. There was just something about the purity and weight of those glass vases that I loved.

On one of our first dates, we had stumbled across an eccentric little shop in Laguna Beach, California, that sold handblown artisan crystal. At first glance, I had fallen in love with a piece that I believed I had to have and ended up spending *way* too much money to bring back to Nashville. There was a purplish glow in the glass—it was as beautiful as any vase I had ever seen.

When I walked past the case after our mediation meeting, I instantly knew it was the most valuable and significant thing I owned that represented our relationship, since I bought it on one of our first dates.

Reluctantly, I grabbed the vase and decided to make it a part of this new collection. As I stood on the concrete floor of the garage, I placed the first item inside the pillowcase and twisted the mouth of the fabric tight. I started praying, telling God I was letting go of the past as I slammed each item—one by one—down on the floor again and again. I smashed the contents as if I were standing at some kind of sacrificial altar. I have to tell you—it felt great!

Finally, I came to the final item—the beautiful vase that I loved. That prayer went a bit longer, because in all transparency, I found it considerably harder to offer up something in which I still found beauty and value. I remember my prayer quite well. "God, I don't want to give this up, but I am going to. I am *so angry* I even have to be in this situation at all!"

I then placed the vase inside the pillowcase and threw it onto the concrete floor. But I didn't hear a smash like I did with the other items. This was more of a thud. I opened the case to find that the vase wasn't smashed. While there were a couple of scratches, it was still intact. In that moment, I felt as if I heard the voice of God saying, "You are bruised and fractured but not destroyed. I am preserving what was most important to you because you surrendered even what was of the most value to you. Now I give it back to you, still beautiful, a little scuffed, but not devastated."

I took that vase back in the house where it still sits to this day in the case. But the value *and* meaning are now different, because God had shown up as I surrendered. He spared the piece of my collection that I valued the most but had offered up to Him. I believe they call that redemption.

You might think God is angry with you now and you're just trying to stay clear of Him. Or you may be angry with God because you feel He allowed the awful things that have happened to you. Go ahead and bring all of that emotion and mess to Him. Don't hold anything back. He can handle it. In Psalms, David lets God hear his complaints. He expressed his disappointment and anger to God, and God even called him a man after His own heart! There are so many examples in the Bible of the heroes of our faith struggling out loud with their Father and even wrestling with angels.

He is not pursuing you so He can get you to say all the "right" things or do some religious dance. He simply wants an authentic, honest, and intimate relationship with you—for better or worse, for richer or poorer, in sickness and in health.

Look at the life of Jesus. He had to handle the cross solo—completely alone. No one else's blood and death would solve the problem of man's sin. In the Gospels, we see three ways He dealt with this pain:

1. *He was honest with God.* As Jesus hung on the cross and was humiliated and beaten for the world to see, He said these words to His Father recorded in Matthew 27:46: "My God, my God, why have you forsaken me?"

Jesus Himself felt horrific mental anguish, despair, and loneliness, and He called out in raw honesty. He felt alone. Rejected. Broken. And He said so, even asking God, "Why?"

2. *He acknowledged His need.* Jesus then acknowledged His human need, recorded in John 19:28-29:

Later, knowing that everything had now been finished, and so that Scripture would be fulfilled, Jesus said, "I am thirsty." A jar of wine vinegar was there, so they soaked a sponge in it, put the sponge on a stalk of the hyssop plant, and lifted it to Jesus' lips.

He called out to anyone who might have mercy that He was literally parched.

3. *He committed Himself to God.* Jesus' final words are found in Luke 23:46: "Jesus called out with a loud voice, 'Father, into your hands I commit my spirit.' When he had said this, he breathed his last."

As we honestly express all of our feelings and needs to our Father just as Jesus did, we then must trust our Father to give us the strength to cross the bridge from anger to peace.

You don't have to clean yourself up and say all the proper words to talk to your heavenly Father. He already knows every thought you have. Healing comes when you discover that God is all right with hearing your raw emotions and know that He draws close to the brokenhearted. He understands your anger and pain.

Here's the bottom line: You need to let the anger out before it does you in.

SOLO CONFESSIONAL

"I have found that if I don't deal with my anger in a healthy manner, I tend to take it out on my kids by being short and impatient with them or just showing a bad attitude. So, for me, working out or going on a walk or run helps release that energy. When I feel myself getting to the place where I know my anger is escalating, I excuse myself and try to change my emotional and mental state."

TINA

Life on the Other Side

This season of being on your own will become the foundation of your future to come. Take your time. Don't hurry through it. A tragic experience can become a beautiful, tender time of knowing just how much God cares for you, not about your social, professional, or marital status.

The foundation you can build for you and your family can be unshakable. The God of the universe, the One who created all things—from the smallest of insects to the greatest of mountains to the complexity of the human mind—is passionately in love with you. He has the power to redeem and rebuild your life, which has been robbed and destroyed by the enemy (John 10:10). He wants you to come to Him so He can cradle you in His arms. God longs to show you how He created you for Himself, that you bring Him pleasure as His child, and that nothing can shake His love for you. He is your Defender and Finisher.

Two Paths: You Choose

When the bottom dropped out of my life, I had some tough choices to face. I could believe my world was falling apart and that life was now over, or I could believe that anything was still possible because God was and is not surprised by my circumstances and is still on His throne. I didn't want to end up mired and sinking into a bitterly hopeless abyss, as I had witnessed among so many others as they walked through divorce.

On this unpleasant journey, we end up either broken

or hardened. These are quite opposite responses. From the outside, they can look very much the same. But inside, we know the difference. One hurts, while the other denies the pain. One is on the road to healing, while the other is deepening the wound. One is open to God and other people, while the other pushes everyone away. That is why taking a serious inventory and honestly assessing which path you're on is vital for positive and healthy change.

You choose to harden yourself or you accept the brokenness: Both are beliefs—a story you tell yourself, a way you live and think.

Hardened people believe life must be lived in defense mode. Just as a pill bug rolls into a ball when it believes danger is near, hardened people subconsciously and constantly stay on guard, ready to "roll up" and show only a shell. These people may shut down, run, or take whatever posture or action they believe will protect them from vulnerability and being hurt again.

Hardened people say life's problems are all someone else's fault, while vowing to never be placed in a bad situation again. So they glue a protective shell strategically onto every aspect of life.

Hardened people believe they can truly rely only on themselves. Others can interact within the surface, but that's all. Even God is held at arm's length. The challenge with this posture is that it will continue to build upon itself. If we're hardened, we may buy the lie of being safe from the effects of others, but we severely limit the opportunity for real intimacy with anyone.

The hardened path was my first choice after my divorce.

Isolating myself from others in the early days felt like the only trustworthy option. It's a natural human reaction.

Eventually, I found the broken path. When we take this path, we believe that we have always been in this broken state because of sin. Therefore, *everyone* is broken. Life circumstances simply can magnify our great need for healing. Being broken is not being weak, but knowing and believing where our real strength comes from. Being broken means we're pliable. It means we realize we are not, and have never been, in control.

During the last few years of my marriage, I felt as if I were swimming upstream against the current. Sometimes I had the sensation of drowning. But when I surrendered to the Lord after the divorce and stopped fighting, peace and rest came, and I simply floated to where He led. When you're in a river, it's important to know the current. Do you want to drown in self-gratification, laziness, apathy, bitterness, and the like? Or do you want to flow easily with God's current? It's critical to distinguish which choice will take you where you need to be. Which choice will lead to healing? What you decide will determine the future for you and your children.

Being still and asking God to direct you on His path and into His flow—wherever that leads—is a clear sign of acknowledging your brokenness. Surrendering and letting Him open the right doors, close the wrong ones, and give you peace about the safe situations while bringing the right people into your life is challenging at first. Divorce by its very nature is about trying to take control of something that has gotten out of control. But trying to control our lives by ourselves is no way to live, no place to stay. Those who have lost a spouse to death will perhaps experience an even more drastic pull to gain control of their world, which suddenly has been turned upside down.

You will have the time and energy one day to rebuild your life. But not until you recognize how much you need this place of stillness right now, to be alone in God's beauty, away from everything—just the two of you in a place of calm, peace, and safety. A place where your deepest intimate need may find fulfillment.

Brokenness is about uncovering our true needs and bringing them to God. We must trust Him with what is next. We can be sure He knows.

Believe me, this broken place was and still is very difficult for me. I am accustomed to making things happen. After all, I started a marketing company when I was twenty-two, a music company at twenty-five, and a media group at forty-one. I have always been up for a challenge. Remaining broken and surrendered is the hardest job I have ever had.

But just as when I launched my companies, getting started was the toughest part. Yet once the endeavor gained traction, challenges still came, but the rewards of the hard work also began to appear. In following the broken path, inertia takes over, habits are forged, and trust is built— proving that staying broken is incredibly rewarding.

Surrender will never be easy. It goes against everything that seems natural, *especially* as a single parent. But believing in self-reliance is deception. The truth is you cannot do surgery on yourself and you alone can't repair, recover, and heal from what you have experienced. To be blunt, you'll eventually bleed out—spiritually, emotionally, and mentally. You can no more sustain yourself than you can live without food. There is simply not enough *you* for that.

Coming to the end of myself while facing my own brokenness brought the moments when I started feeling freedom, empowerment, and hope in a greater way than *ever* before. I gave up trying to carry this giant burden on my own. I rested in the truth that in my weakness, God shows Himself to be strong.

Will you prayerfully read these verses that have helped me so much?

My grace is enough; it's all you need. My strength comes into its own in your weakness. Once I heard that, I was glad to let it happen. I quit focusing on the handicap and began appreciating the gift. It was a case of Christ's strength moving in on my weakness.

2 CORINTHIANS 12:9, MSG

Don't panic. I'm with you. There's no need to fear for I'm your God. I'll give you strength. I'll help you. I'll hold you steady, keep a firm grip on you.

ISAIAH 41:10, MSG

He puts poor people on their feet again; he rekindles burned-out lives with fresh hope, restoring dignity and respect to their lives—a place in the sun! For the very structures of earth are GOD's; he has laid out his operations on a firm foundation.

1 SAMUEL 2:8, MSG

But you, GOD, shield me on all sides; You ground
my feet, you lift my head high; With all my might
I shout up to GOD, His answers thunder from the
holy mountain. I stretch myself out. I sleep. Then
I'm up again—rested, tall and steady, fearless before
the enemy mobs coming at me from all sides.

PSALM 3:3-6, MSG

From my own experience, I know that brokenness is the
only gateway to our Father, His promises, and healing for
our families and us. I *know* this to be true—as sure as I am
certain that the sun will rise each morning.

You are not alone. He is here. Do you need a miracle? If
you choose the path of brokenness that leads to God, yours
is on the way.

4

FIRST STEPS TO A NEW LIFE

AT THE END OF MY MARRIAGE, I had a few good friends who were so amazing, supportive, and reassuring. They constantly encouraged me by saying, "You'll be okay," "What matters now is taking care of yourself and the girls," "If there is anything I can do to help, I'm here." But even with all their care and comfort, nothing took away the ache in my heart.

As I was attempting to begin some form of recovery, I was confiding in my pastor friend, Father Thomas. He and I had become close, so he invited me to join him at a Samson Society meeting.

Finding Community

The Samson Society is a Christian fellowship of men who get together regularly and share their secrets—drinking,

porn, prostitutes, drugs, embezzling—the kinds of things
men deal with but never talk about.

I felt a freedom to share my story in that circle, and I
received love, support, and acceptance, along with assurance that I wouldn't have to bear this pain alone. While
I was married, I had attended some support groups for
people dealing with substance abuse in their families.
The Samson Society was different—I connected with
it more since it wasn't focused only on a disease. Guys
would bring *all* of their struggles to the table at these
meetings.

I found the equivalent of a "sponsor" in the Samson
Society, and I checked in with him at least once a day.
These were my first serious steps toward self-care and
receiving support. Those guys went to court with me,
called me, and had my back. And I had theirs.

For the first time in my life, I started to understand the
value of community. After God created Adam, He said, "It is
not good for the man to be alone" (Genesis 2:18). My entire
life I had insulated myself from deep meaningful relationships for fear of trusting someone. I was beginning to understand why God would make such a statement about us. He
didn't intend for our lives to be lived alone. Even though
intimacy with our God is the only way to reach health and
wholeness, sharing that journey with others is also part of
His plan.

I was also starting to understand that there is a real purpose for seeking a mate. I could now see why Jesus Himself
traveled in a community much of His life. Mary and
Martha were just as close to Him as Peter and John were.

Intimate and quite human friends were an everyday part of Christ's divine life. My dear friends Jordyn and Nina along with Nate and Thomas provided the companionship I needed at the beginning of my solo days.

In this season of brokenness, I was continually reminded that I was not alone. Men in my brotherhood were not afraid to own their own brokenness, and that somehow soothed mine. Women friends helped and supported my daughters, and our friendship became even closer.

Some of the practical principles I learned during this time had to do with the company we keep and where we receive our emotional and spiritual support.

In community, we are:

Defined—Who we are can be known by others.

> Dear friends, since God so loved us, we also ought
> to love one another. No one has ever seen God;
> but if we love one another, God lives in us and his
> love is made complete in us. This is how we know
> that we live in him and he in us: He has given us
> of his Spirit.
>
> 1 JOHN 4:11-13

Intertwined—What we do affects others.

> Dear children, let us not love with words or speech
> but with actions and in truth. This is how we know
> that we belong to the truth and how we set our
> hearts at rest in his presence.
>
> 1 JOHN 3:18-19

Refined—Where we take our lives can change us for the good to benefit others.

> Each one of us should please our neighbors for
> their good, to build them up. For even Christ
> did not please himself but, as it is written:
> "The insults of those who insult you have
> fallen on me."
>
> ROMANS 15:2-3

Facing Regrets and Ghosts

Do you ever wonder why—despite the trauma surrounding your divorce or separation— you sometimes can find yourself missing or even wanting your spouse back?

When I was being completely honest with myself, I certainly had those moments. I was not expecting this to happen and the emotions always seemed to surprise me. Our raw human feelings can be comforting and conflicting all at the same time.

Even though I felt devastated, often I wanted her back. Though I tried, I couldn't reconcile the feelings. Why should I find myself missing her? Not just from sentimentality, but legitimately wanting her back in my life. Wanting *us* back. While I had grown accustomed to dealing with contradiction and viewing both sides of every coin, these feelings totally stumped me.

How could I possibly want to invite the chaos back into my life? Why did I want what caused so much pain to return? This made no sense, but our feelings so often defy all logic.

Recognizing the Wound

First responders warn, while at the scene of an accident, about the danger of removing a foreign object that has punctured a victim's body, and how extreme care in extracting it has to be administered for the person to survive.

When the body is punctured by anything invasive such as a pole, rod, or sharp object, it usually goes in quickly by a smooth motion, creating a wound its exact size. This object acts as a plug to the injury, with the blood vessels that are cut being pressed into and dammed up by the object itself. Improper extraction can not only create severe bleeding, but also cause the damaged part of the body to collapse.

This is why you see first responders at the scene of an accident leave the object in the victim's body, cutting it away from its source to stabilize it in the person during transport to a hospital. Often, EMTs and paramedics will secure it by wrapping thick bandages around the object and the wound, attempting to hold it in place. But the object will need removal once adequate medical care is available.

Understanding this rule of physical first aid might keep us from returning to relationships that are destructive to us emotionally and mentally, as well as understanding our need for healing from the extraction.

When we have a toxic relationship in our lives, we can learn to function, often creating a new norm, making allowance for the damage of the wound. When that person is removed from our lives, this can essentially create a painful space or what feels like a lethal collapse of the heart. This is exactly why we believe everything in our world is caving in around us—even if the person being removed never should have been there in the first place.

Whether physically or emotionally, removing the offending source is serious business. In order for a human to survive and live in health, the wounds left from a toxic relationship or the death of a spouse must eventually receive treatment, but that treatment requires great care and expertise.

SOLO CONFESSIONAL

"When my husband and I divorced, I often described our relationship as me having a third arm. Sometimes the arm was very useful, but more often than not, it was obtrusive. I was embarrassed by it and didn't like the extra arm. So after some years of struggling with this situation, I got rid of my third arm. However, ironically, I sometimes missed having it. Despite how much I didn't like the extra arm, it could be helpful at times and I had grown accustomed to having it there. Not long after I got rid of it, though, someone else picked up my third arm and took it over as theirs. Even though I didn't *really* want it back, I still felt like someone had taken something from me. This made me sad. Such are the conflicting emotions after a divorce. Relief and resolve on one hand; regret and sadness on the other."

JORDAN

The "knife in our back" cannot stay lodged there if we are ever to be healthy, even if our emotions and feelings have "grown around it" and we have convinced ourselves we can function normally. Well, we can't. Too many of us who are now solo walk around with a gaping wound from the sudden removal of a relationship, bleeding from the extraction, caving in from the void, but no attention has been given toward true healing.

A healthy and refreshed perspective can give us the comfort we need in knowing that something has to change. We must see things as they *are*, not as we *hope* they would be or could be. Ignoring the problem will kill your spirit—eventually. This is certainly a slow death, but a death all the same.

Healing from Toxins

To heal, we must employ accountability to remove each and every destructive element in our lives and have the patience to let the process of healing take place. And it is indeed a process, never a quick fix. These can include any issue we brought into our marriage that contributed to its failure, as well as any that manifested inside the marriage that we still carry today.

We are all hurting and fallen people, so we *will* bring baggage and dysfunction into all relationships. When the partners in a marriage become toxic and selfish, not only do they tend *not* to deal with past issues, but they also create new ones. In a healthy relationship where continual growth and maturity are the goals of both spouses, a couple can actually address and rid themselves of past issues brought into the union. The point here is health builds on health as dysfunction builds on dysfunction. Nothing changes if nothing changes.

The following questions/exercises helped me face the dilemma of missing the toxicity and taking steps toward healing. I encourage you to set aside some time to prayerfully work through these.

- Focus on one thing your former spouse did that was destructive. Just one. Recall and write down all your feelings regarding that incident or issue. The goal here is not to drudge up bad memories but to process your emotions about the damage created.

- Self-care requires you move away from a destructive mind-set. Write down one thing you can do or change on a daily basis to deal positively with your wounds. An example of this for me was processing the shame by reflecting on the truth of how God sees me.

- Consider how your spouse filled the need in your life for companionship. Write down how you can, in a healthy manner, cautiously begin to address your need for relationships in this season. In my life, I began to share this need with men who were close to me.

- Realize that the longing for your ex-spouse may actually be a desire to fill the emptiness you feel. Try to describe your need and any feelings associated with the void left from your spouse's absence.

- Believe that God will be faithful to give you what you need in His timing. Write down exactly, specifically, what you want and most desire to see God do in this season and in your new life.

- Take some time to pray, honestly and openly, with thoughts like, *God, I am broken. I feel alone and empty. I need you to replace the love I have lost with your Fatherly care. You say You will never leave me or forsake me. Give me the strength to believe You. I need You now more than ever.*

God already knows what you think, so you may as well be completely honest with Him.

There were days I would curl up on my bed and weep as the despair and questions overwhelmed me. Shaking uncontrollably, the cry came deep from my core. Feeling so abandoned and broken, I saw no way out or through. I would cry out to God, "Why?" "I can't do this!" "How could she?"

King David certainly gave us a crash course in how to be gut-level honest when praying, and God always responded to his transparency. If you're concerned about God being able to handle your honesty, consider David's thoughts:

Long enough, GOD—you've ignored me long enough.
I've looked at the back of your head long enough.
Long enough I've carried this ton of trouble, lived
with a stomach full of pain. Long enough my arrogant
enemies have looked down their noses at me. Take a

good look at me, GOD, my God; I want to look life in
the eye, so no enemy can get the best of me or laugh
when I fall on my face.

PSALM 13:1-4, MSG

Through the Valley

When I was alone and feeling insecure I felt the most
exposed and vulnerable. This situation had both good and
bad outcomes. There were moments where time alone
fostered a great intimacy with my Father, but then others
where the space turned into what David called "the valley of the shadow of death" in Psalm 23 (KJV). In those
times, not only was my soul deep in grief, but I also felt
as though the shadow of death was hovering over me.

This dark place feels like a blank space where *everything* can seem uncertain. Living in the limbo of knowing
something bad is about to take place and unable to do
anything about it is terrifying and exhausting. For me, so
many aspects of life felt like they were in suspense. I had
constant questions such as . . .

- How am I going to do all this alone?
- Will I be able to stay in this house?
- Will the kids be able to stay in the same school?
- How can I work full-time and be there for the girls?
- Am I always going to feel this lonely and isolated?
- Are people going to view me as a failure?
- Am I now destined to go through the rest of my life
  without a spouse?

These questions grew deafeningly loud when I was alone.

All my life, especially as a missionary kid, I had heard Psalm 23. During those early months of my solo season, the words became my lifeline to stay sane and keep moving forward.

> The LORD is my shepherd;
> I shall not want.
> He makes me to lie down in green pastures;
> He leads me beside the still waters.
> He restores my soul;
> He leads me in the paths of righteousness
> For His name's sake.
> Yea, though I walk through the valley of the
> shadow of death,
> I will fear no evil;
> For You are with me;
> Your rod and Your staff, they comfort me.
>
> PSALM 23:1-4, NKJV

In these legendary phrases, I find it interesting that David begins by referring to God as "The LORD," but later addresses Him directly, personally. And where does he move toward this intimacy? When talking about "the valley of the shadow of death."

So often, I prayed that God would remove me from my darkest valleys. I begged Him to fix my situation by delivering me back to the mountaintop where I wanted to live, where I had been in those early days of my marriage.

But sometimes the valley is exactly the place where God

works most in our lives. He fixes us *in* the situation. He doesn't take us *out*; He sees us *through*. He doesn't change the circumstances for us; He changes us in the circumstances.

This understanding reoriented me to a new knowledge of how God sees me as His cherished son. The Bible never promises that He will keep us out of the valley, but what He does promise is He is with us *through* the valley. The word *through* is very important in this passage. David doesn't say this is where we stay or set up camp. We are walking *through*—and God is with us, always and intimately.

These words also became my declaration, used in repetition during my time of meditation in prayer—"I will not fear. You are with me."

You, too, can claim this divine message. These promises are found throughout the Bible.

Just before she passed away, my mom made a video with final messages to her kids and grandkids. Her specific message to me as I was in the middle of *my solo season* was this verse:

> Don't panic. I'm with you. There's no need to fear for I'm your God. I'll give you strength. I'll help you. I'll hold you steady, keep a firm grip on you.
>
> ISAIAH 41:10, MSG

The Escalator Effect

On a trip to Italy, I went hiking on the Isle of Capri—completely unintentionally. The person I was with wanted to see the famous Faraglioni stacks, three towering rock formations jutting out from the Mediterranean Sea, just off the island's coast.

When we reached the side of the cliff, we looked over and there they were—massive creations formed by the sea's erosion. They were fascinatingly beautiful. Next to where we were standing, a sign marked the beginning of a trail that went down the sheer cliff—300 meters. My travel partner lit up and said, "Let's go!" Although I protested, because I'm not an avid outdoorsman or hiker, my words were in vain.

Within moments, we were on the trail headed down to the base of the colossal formations. I was happy to find that, much of the way, there were stairs laid into the side of the steep path making the trek a bit easier. But the return trip required walking up those same steep stairs.

While the hike down was definitely worth the close-up view of the stacks, the hike up seemed to take forever. The steps . . . just . . . kept . . . coming. The journey upward began to feel as if I were walking up the down escalator, walking in place and gaining no ground.

But the hike was worth it because I discovered a dynamic that helped me navigate my new life. When I focused on my surroundings, namely the seemingly unending stairs I still had to climb to get to the top, I felt hopeless, questioning if I could make it. This perspective only compounded my exhaustion and made me feel overwhelmed and defeated. But when I kept my head down and focused only on the next step right in front of me, knowing each one I scaled brought me closer to my destination, then my spirit, as well as my exhaustion, began to lift.

As I thought about how each one of those steps had been

carved and laid to help me, that they were deliberately set there by someone so I could see this beautiful place, I lost track of how many steps were left to take. I just took one at a time, appreciating both the step provided as well as the progress I made.

Managing your inner voices and navigating the countless questions in "the valley of the shadow of death" is best done by looking at each step—one at a time. When we look at the entire shadow hovering above, we will always be overwhelmed. When we look only at what is right in front of us, we'll find it easier to trust where God is leading.

Our valleys are mere seasons that exist only in sharp contrast to the mountains on either side. Life in the valley is not permanent; it's a turning point. Yet, we are still climbing the exhausting trek upward to our new life, accepting the new normal. While temporary, this is an important journey toward eternal change.

I had far too many days when I fought my new normal, when I tried to figure out every "what if" question immediately. And every time I would entertain the many "what ifs," I would panic. I was looking up at all the steps still to come, thinking I couldn't make it. And you know what? I couldn't. Still can't. But that is why God is God and I am not.

In my new normal, I accepted that although I was continually surprised, God never was. Fighting our circumstances in the valley only cripples our ability to start building a new life.

On many days, I felt the escalator effect—I was moving but didn't seem to be making progress. Yet even on those days, I had to release the step from the day before, the one

I could no longer do anything about. And every day, I had to keep myself from jumping ahead to the next day's step because that took my focus off the one right in front of me. The only step I needed to take for that day was the one God placed before me. This mind-set is the path to true progress.

Some days it took all of my effort to get out of bed and take care of the girls. On other days, I felt very productive. I was careful, though, not to measure the days against each other. I knew that each day was equally critical to making progress, just as each step up the cliff in Italy was important.

Each step of rehabilitation, rest, and rebuilding you take will be helpful during your solo parenting season.

Rehabilitation—healing and self-care

As solo parents, we are so often walking wounded. While life has to go on, we must take any step possible to bring healing and take care of ourselves to be healthy for our lives and our children. Church small groups, counseling, circles of close friends and family can all be conduits to rehabilitation. And we must also remember when people enter any sort of rehab, there is a strong belief they can and will be healthy and whole again.

Rest—stopping and being still

In this context, rest is more than a Sunday afternoon nap or sleeping in on Saturday. It's a recharge of your spiritual and mental energy, the way to replenish the emotional and physical exhaustion that constantly plagues most single parents. There is a type of rest only God can give us deep in our spirits that can provide us with a fresh perspective on our reality.

Rebuilding—taking new steps toward new life

Rebuilding is much like peeling an onion. You peel an onion one layer at a time; you rebuild one step at a time. When we give God our lives, He will give us our new steps. Unfortunately, there is no elevator to a new life, but by God's mercy and grace we take one step after another toward what He alone can build in us and in our children.

While there is no particular order or magic balance for these three R's, each step is important and useful for moving forward. Realizing which step you are on in the moment can keep you from feeling overwhelmed. Value each step for its own uniqueness, placed there with care to take you where you need to be.

And, as parents, we must always follow the flight attendant's advice: "If you are traveling with your child, secure your oxygen mask first, and then assist your child." We must constantly work on our own rehabilitation, rest, and rebuilding so we can give our kids our very best and secure a bright future for them.

SOLO PARENT PRINCIPLE

While the great need for the constant care of your children is a top priority, you must keep in the forefront of your mind that the healthier you become, the healthier they can also become. Any help and support you receive for yourself will be funneled back into their lives as well. You can't give what you don't have.

Building Your New Life

As we close this chapter, let's return to our invasive object analogy and ask these questions: Was your spouse suddenly removed from your life? Have you struggled to cope, wanting him or her back, sometimes even much to your own confusion and questioning? Is the wound collapsing, affecting your health in every area of life? Do you need help from someone to stop the bleeding?

Are you in the healing process, free from the relationship, but still taking one step at a time to climb to your new life? What do you need to spur you on and keep you on track to complete health and success? Specifically, what are you doing to rehabilitate, rest, and rebuild?

Regardless of where you are in your journey, even though you may struggle to believe it now, your new life is being built with *each step* you take. You might feel as if you're only crawling, but even so, you are heading toward a stronger life, a better life, a life you may have only dreamed of before.

The following verses might help you as you begin taking steps to your new life:

The LORD makes firm the steps of the one who
delights in him.

PSALM 37:23

Direct my footsteps according to your word;
let no sin rule over me.

PSALM 119:133

In their hearts humans plan their course, but
the LORD establishes their steps.

PROVERBS 16:9

A person's steps are directed by the LORD. How
then can anyone understand their own way?

PROVERBS 20:24

There's an opportune time to do things, a right
time for everything on the earth:

A right time for birth and another for death,
A right time to plant and another to reap,
A right time to kill and another to heal,
A right time to destroy and another to construct,
A right time to cry and another to laugh,
A right time to lament and another to cheer,
A right time to make love and another to abstain,
A right time to embrace and another to part,
A right time to search and another to count your losses,
A right time to hold on and another to let go,
A right time to rip out and another to mend,
A right time to shut up and another to speak up,
A right time to love and another to hate,
A right time to wage war and another to make peace.

ECCLESIASTES 3:1-8, MSG

5

DECIDING TO DANCE

As WITH SO MANY OF us on this solo road, the years prior to divorce are often rocky and even on-again, off-again. In my situation, my ex had actually filed for divorce years before it became official.

We made every attempt to reconcile. We even flew to Rome once to renew our vows in a beautiful basilica. It's interesting how we can attempt to create grand mountaintop moments to overcome life lived in the darkest of valleys.

Each time we would promise to work things out but then end up right back where we were. Of course, while I understood what was happening, my children did not. These adult circumstances just created confusion and chaos for them, and the relational ping-pong effect was devastating.

Reaching Release

Following our divorce, the methodical, gradual steps I started taking alone, such as being deliberate about spending quiet time with God, were leading me to a new and unexpected place. My first realization of this was the moment I knew I was free from any heart connection with my ex.

It happened during an unexpected meeting with her outside of a restaurant in the pouring rain. At first, I was angry about the circumstances and that my ex-wife was even there. And then my frustration left me. I realized I was now viewing my ex and her life from a different perspective

In that moment, I also noticed something new for the first time. That place in my heart where she had been for so long was at peace with the vacancy. My personal attachment was . . . gone. I wasn't expecting this test, but I certainly passed.

For the first time, I felt nothing for her as my ex-wife. But for the hurting person standing in front of me, I felt a deep compassion.

You will *know* when you are truly set free from the relationship. People always say when you meet the right person, you'll "just know." I think the moment you realize a relationship is finished, you also "just know." The former is fun, exciting, and full of wonder. The latter provides just a sense of relinquishment and relief, but also gratefulness, since you can now truly move forward.

When you feel released from your past relationship, it doesn't mean you don't care about the welfare of the person. It does mean your emotions are no longer tied to or affected by him or her. For me, the unexpected meeting with my ex-spouse was a defining moment that signaled my readiness to move on.

Little g, Big G

Let's discuss an issue that many people deal with in their marriages and divorces, an issue that I'd call an epidemic in our culture. It's codependency. If you haven't noticed it by now, I am a recovering, card-carrying codependent person.

If you are codependent, you rely excessively on another person to meet most of your emotional and self-esteem needs and to provide approval and a sense of identity. Codependency is a relationship in which one person enables another's dysfunction—whether it's an addiction, under-achievement, or irresponsibility—and places the needs of another before his or her own.

When we attach our own well-being to the emotions and actions of someone else, we will always be disappointed. Ironically, codependent people tend to remain in the relationship, thinking the *next* interaction will finally be the time when everything works. This occurs because we make the other person our god. We can be codependent with or make a god out of a . . .

- spouse
- child
- parent
- friend

We can even become codependent on a life factor such as . . .

- career
- status
- wealth
- appearance

The Bible is clear about who alone may have this place in our lives: "You shall have no other gods before me" (Exodus 20:3).

God did not give this command because He is a cosmic narcissist. He told us this because He knows if we find our source anywhere else—in anyone else or in anything else— we will never experience wholeness.

Let's face it. You and I, along with everyone we know, make lousy gods. When we attempt to give ourselves or anyone else this position, we just end up striving to fulfill a need that can *never* be satisfied by a person or a thing. In the same way that placing security in someone else is futile, we ourselves must realize that we are not enough to change anyone else. There *really is* no other God.

Israel found this out the hard way: First the Israelites invented a new god; later they made the mistake of demanding a king.

> All the elders of Israel gathered together and came to
> Samuel at Ramah. They said to him, "You are old,
> and your sons do not follow your ways; now appoint

a king to lead us, such as all the other nations have."
But when they said, "Give us a king to lead us," this
displeased Samuel; so he prayed to the LORD. And
the LORD told him: "Listen to all that the people are
saying to you; it is not you they have rejected, but
they have rejected me as their king. As they have done
from the day I brought them up out of Egypt until
this day, forsaking me and serving other gods, so they
are doing to you. Now listen to them; but warn them
solemnly and let them know what the king who will
reign over them will claim as his rights."

I SAMUEL 8:4-9

Throughout our lives, most of us have replaced God with
another god in various seasons and situations. We've placed
a person, a thing, or something intangible on the throne of
our lives. We must remember the principle found in this
passage. Saying "yes" to a new god or king of our hearts is
also saying "no" to the God who can save us, redeem us,
and heal us. The focus here is not so much on whom we
are accepting as whom we are rejecting.

In that unexpected meeting with my ex-wife, I gave up
my "little 'g' god," releasing my ex and our relationship. It
was as if the rain pouring from the sky that evening was
symbolically cleansing my spirit and baptizing me into
new life.

That unplanned event was the first time I realized that I
could not heal my ex-wife's pain. I was not the solution.
I had always believed *I* was the answer. Yet on this night,
I saw so clearly that I was not, and never would be.

> ## SOLO PARENT PRINCIPLE
> Once the divorce is final, *every* decision must be about what is best for the children. We can easily manipulate or mask a choice as being best for the kids when it is actually connected more to our ex or us. Consider any decision carefully to be certain the kids are the real focus and priority.

Healthy Boundaries

This "aha moment" is a critical milestone for any solo parent. Establishing and enforcing healthy boundaries with a former spouse is crucial to healing. I wish I had learned this truth much earlier. Before the divorce, the girls were never sure of what our home was going to be like from one day to the next. I can only imagine what life must have been like for them in those days. I have thought many times that if only I could return to the girls' younger days, I would try to have the strength to end the detrimental patterns my ex and I had established in our home.

In a counseling session during our marriage, I recall hearing about setting boundaries. At that time, I had committed to using them, but somehow when the moment came to actually set one up, I would fall back and not use the tools I had been given. Now I can see clearly that a codependent person can take steps toward health for each parent and, most especially, for the children.

In our local Solo Parent Society groups, we discuss boundaries and their importance.

One of our group members, Kendra, struggled with creating enough boundaries to help her and her kids move on from the past. Two of them have medical problems, so she allowed visitation with her ex-husband in her home. She didn't want to leave him alone with the children, so she stayed in the house during visitation. She and her ex went together to family campouts, Cub Scouts, and football games. The kids saw their parents together so much that it made it much harder for them to transition to separate homes. Looking back, she realizes she should have limited the time with her ex. She has since worked on establishing a healthy boundary of separation.

In another example, when Brian saw his ex-wife failing, he often ran in and rescued her, creating an unhealthy cycle of having to always "save the day." We must realize it is important to let the kids see the situation for what it is without us making excuses, hiding, or minimizing what is happening. The obvious exception is never leaving our kids in a dangerous situation. Brian had to learn how to build a boundary, restraining himself from saving his ex-wife from her dilemmas for the sake of his kids. He no longer feels responsibility to tend to all of the situations. Instead he prays, "God, go get her. It's on You now, not me."

Sometimes boundaries have to be established even around the good intentions of others. One widow in our group told us that she had to set one with well-meaning family members who wanted her and her children to move back to her hometown. They were constantly offering how they could help with the kids. While their advice and assistance was welcome to her, it was important for this widow to choose her boundaries. Telling her relatives she was not moving was hard to do but an important step.

She shared, "Accepting respite help is a godsend, but I had to define what my terms were. I had to ask myself, *Am I willing to move? How often am I comfortable with other people in my house cleaning or cooking without feeling our family space is being invaded?*

Everyone in our Solo Parent Society group agreed that creating a healthy boundary around the drop-off of kids to an ex-spouse is of the utmost importance. They've learned that it's healthiest to plan a simple and transactional exchange, one that avoids anything except politely handing off the children. This idea was echoed strongly by a counselor who encourages the handoff to be viewed almost as much of a nonevent as ordering at a fast-food drive-through. A simple yes, no, and thank-you is hard to engage with, said Sissy Goff on a Solo Parent Society podcast.[1] You shouldn't have to do more than that.

Keep in mind that boundaries should not be used to isolate ourselves. We need others. Consider fences; they have two purposes—keeping things in and keeping things out. Also, we add gates along the fence lines in the places where we will need frequent access outside the boundary.

One solo parent in our group said that guilt prompted her to create an unhealthy boundary. If she wasn't able to "repay" people who offered her assistance, this parent felt guilty. Instead of accepting this type of help, she decided to prove she could do life alone. She wanted to show that she could "hold everything together." When she realized that this false boundary could negatively affect her and her kids, she worked at overcoming it, allowing and accepting legitimate help.

Solo Confessional

"For many years, Robert has been one of my close friends and I had walked through his ordeal with him. Then my own marriage took a tragic turn when I discovered my wife was a 'secret' or 'closet' alcoholic. Our boys were old enough to see what was happening and the damage this was causing us all. One night at a restaurant, my oldest son looked me straight in the eyes and implored, "Dad, what are you going to do about Mom?" In that moment, he was both making me responsible for a solution and letting me know he needed me to do something— sooner than later. Unfortunately, my wife's choices forced me down a path of becoming solo myself."

RUSTY

In All Things

While we need to set healthy boundaries with our former spouses, we also need to maintain compassion and grace for them. There is a saying that rose from the church in the 1600s that the Methodist Church still uses today: "In essentials, unity; in nonessentials, liberty; and in all things, charity." This phrase describes the difference between essential doctrine in the church and elements that are simply preferential and nonconsequential to the maintenance and growth of the church at large. Our reactions to differing priorities must be rooted in "charity" or Christ's love.

Here's a modified version of this motto for solo parents to live by: "In families, unity; in broken families, liberty; and in all things, charity." Unity is the goal, freedom is available, and love is essential. Regardless of our specific situations, we can all agree this approach sets up the *best* environment for our children.

> When I was a child, I talked like a child, I thought like a child, I reasoned like a child. When I became a man, I put the ways of childhood behind me. For now we see only a reflection as in a mirror; then we shall see face to face. Now I know in part; then I shall know fully, even as I am fully known. And now these three remain: faith, hope and love. But the greatest of these is love.
>
> I CORINTHIANS 13:11-13

God's intention for families is for them to be together forever—period. This mind-set serves everyone best. Unity models and reflects the union we have in a relationship with Christ.

When the bond of the family is severed, we can create a new baseline if we surrender and acknowledge our broken state and engage in the restoration process with our heavenly Father. When we do this, we can release the burdens we carry. No matter the circumstances, we are called to charity and unity, to faith, hope, and love.

I love the definition of charity—"benevolent goodwill toward or love of humanity, lenient judgment of others, generosity and helpfulness especially toward the suffering."[2] As Christians, God's commands always apply to our treatment of *all* others—even ex-spouses. Nothing will teach our children charity as our own consistent example, especially in difficult circumstances.

> I've told you these things for a purpose: that my joy might be your joy, and your joy wholly mature. This is my command: Love one another the way I loved you. This is the very best way to love. Put your life on the line for your friends. You are my friends when you do the things I command you. I'm no longer calling you servants because servants don't understand what their master is thinking and planning. No, I've named you friends because I've let you in on everything I've heard from the Father. You didn't choose me, remember; I chose you, and put you in the world to bear fruit, fruit that won't spoil. As fruit bearers, whatever you ask the Father in relation to me, he gives you. But remember the root command: Love one another.
>
> JOHN 15:11-17, MSG

Truthfully, there have been many times—and still are—when extending charity has felt almost impossible for me. I wish I could say that I've always felt that sense of grace toward my ex that I did on the evening in the rain. But plenty of times I haven't felt that way.

I've needed to be in court several times every year for

almost a decade. Because of this, I have certainly found it both difficult and challenging to embrace the idea that the foundation of my view regarding my ex must be charity. However, I believe and know God's ways are best and higher, so this is always my goal, though I fail. I want to encourage you to join me in the commitment to charity—even when it seems impossible. But this is exactly *why* we need God.

The New Testament writers often used a phrase that has been translated as "make every effort." God knows we are going to try and then fail in so many areas of life, but He also knows that if we do not attempt obedience, we will never succeed. Therefore, we are encouraged to "make every effort."

> Let us therefore *make every effort* to do what leads to peace and to mutual edification.
> ROMANS 14:19, EMPHASIS ADDED

> *Make every effort* to keep the unity of the Spirit through the bond of peace.
> EPHESIANS 4:3, EMPHASIS ADDED

> *Make every effort* to live in peace with everyone and to be holy.
> HEBREWS 12:14, EMPHASIS ADDED

> Dear friends, since you are looking forward to this, *make every effort* to be found spotless, blameless and at peace with him.
> 2 PETER 3:14, EMPHASIS ADDED

God also knows the best thing for us is to see our ex-spouse as He sees him or her—broken, imperfect, and in need of our Savior, just as we are. It's absolutely vital for our kids and for their other parent that we maintain this worldview.

SOLO PARENT PRINCIPLE

Spouses may get divorced, but parents never do. Work hard to separate your attitude about your ex from your approach to your *children's* other parent so you can maintain a healthy perspective in all you say and do with your kids. For example, when I talked about the girls' mother I worked hard always to be positive.

Children Don't Divorce

Psychologists tell us that no matter the drama surrounding separation and divorce, our children will always see *both* parents as a part of themselves. Always. We might be able to separate ourselves mentally and emotionally from our ex, but our kids are forever a part of both parents.

Harvard Professor Dr. John Chirban did a study of more than 10,000 children and parents of divorce for his book *Collateral Damage*. During an interview for the Solo Parent Society podcast, Chirban told me that the study's two primary "takeaways" on the effect of divorce on children were:

- Kids feel their family is over.
- Kids feel their childhood is over.

Instead of connecting divorce with the word *end*, Chirban suggested parents say "Our family is in transition."[3]

Our kids' identities are tied to both parents, which is why a child will equate our view of our ex as our view of the child. Our children assume that how we treat, speak of, and view our ex is also how we view them. If we apply this emotional truth, we'll understand that when we attack our ex in front of the children, we are in turn attacking our children. Ironically, we may consider what we do or say about the other parent as a way of protecting our child, when in reality our words and actions produce the opposite effect in our child's heart.

I have always made bedtime prayers a part of the girls' nightly ritual, and in the early days of our divorce, I would make sure that we prayed for their mother each evening. I also chose my words carefully, always interceding for her well-being, safety, and happiness. When speaking of, or praying for our ex, we are also modeling what we think of our children.

When the girls asked questions about their mom, I tried to make a habit of being intentional with my answer, taking the time to recognize that, subtly, they were asking how they were doing as well. Slowing down and focusing effort to carefully handle questions about the other parent demonstrates that we care about and respect our children, not only because we provide answers, but also because we are placing a priority on the question.

A mom in our Solo Parent Society group described her approach to speaking about her ex. "It can be easy to be bitter in regards to my ex-husband," she said. "I've found that it helps to select words and phrases that only focus on the positive. Even the word 'ex' has a negative connotation, focusing on what he wouldn't or didn't provide. Using the word 'dad' has a positive connotation, referencing what he always will be, no matter what happens between us. When I refer to him as the boys' dad, I find that my tone and overall attitude are more appropriate than when I refer to him as my ex. I know our kids feel the weight of how we view the situation, so as best as we can, we need to release them from the burden *they* carry about the hurt *we* have felt."

Unexpected, Undeserved Gift

Before we can show grace and compassion to others, including our ex, we must first completely grasp the concept ourselves. One of the most pivotal experiences of my life was the moment I began to understand grace. And this moment occurred because the Christians around me displayed God's gifts of charity, unity, liberty, and grace.

One of my daughters has the middle name Grace. When we named her, I was definitely in a season when I desperately needed God's grace because I knew how recklessly I had been living at the time. This heavenly gift was demonstrated to me during a time in my life that I was living irresponsibly and selfishly, to say the least. I'm not at all proud of my actions during the late evening hours of September 11 and the early morning hours of September 12, 2002, but this is one night I hope never to forget.

Some dear friends and I spontaneously decided to celebrate a birthday further into the evening than we

had originally planned. We had met for drinks at about
5:00 p.m., and at around 8:00 p.m. we called for a limo to
drive us around the rest of the night. We kept celebrating—
and drinking—for several hours before finally getting back
at around 2:00 a.m. to the place we had left our cars.

By this time, I was drunk—very drunk. My behavior
was not fitting for any executive, but most certainly not
for one in Christian music. For some reason I and another
friend of mine, who was also inebriated, thought it would
be a funny gag to "key" the promotional van of a promi-
nent Christian artist.

For anyone who is not well versed in the ways of
vandalism, "keying" is running a key or other sharp
metal object down the side of a vehicle, effectively ruin-
ing the paint job and causing an unsightly scratch that
requires considerable expense and labor to fix. This
musician—TobyMac—was also a friend of mine, but the
record label he recorded with was, by my view, a competitor to my label. So, in a drunken stupor, we "keyed"
TobyMac's van, unaware that a security camera video-
taped the whole incident.

I didn't even remember committing the crime; black-
outs are one of the many results of alcohol abuse. In fact,
I did not remember driving home that night. I have no
recollection about what happened from some point in the
evening until I woke up the next morning.

Weeks later, another friend in the music business gently
approached me at a restaurant, asking, "Hey, Robert,
where were you on the night of September 12?" Uncertain,
I looked at my calendar and saw a meeting in Los Angeles

covering that entire day. While true, this did not include midnight to 2:00 a.m. that day.

But an odd thing occurred in that moment. Suddenly, the memory flooded back. I was filled with terror, regret, and shame. I was so busted and so embarrassed.

I quickly made an appointment to sit down with my "competitor," Greg Ham, and confess what I had done. I realized that I could lose everything from a career stand point. If this news went public, it would ruin my name in Christian music. Even in the Christian marketplace, many people would have used this opportunity to crush an opponent. I felt like a gladiator lying on the ground, waiting for the victor's final swing of the sword after the thumbs-down from the king.

But this man decided I was not his opponent. I was, instead, his brother in Christ. Greg could have destroyed my reputation and taken my livelihood, but he looked me straight in the eyes and said, "Robert, I forgive you." Then he continued, "In fact, I will make sure no one at my company mentions what happened. This issue is in the past." Greg closed by praying for me and handing me his Bible.

This stunned me. I was speechless and utterly disarmed. Greg's response to my sin went against all my instincts of drive and ambition. I could not grasp such an unconditional and unmerited response.

I deserved to be brought down from the seat of glory, the seat I thought I occupied. I should have been publicly humiliated and punished, but what I got instead was intimate mercy, grace, and love. In that moment I was

given a gift—the gift of a welcoming arm and embrace—
much like the Prodigal Son received from his father after
returning home, his inheritance squandered. I received
what I didn't deserve, much like the thief on the cross
who was assured by Christ that he would be ushered into
heaven. When we are at our worst, grace is hard to grasp
and even harder to accept.

But this is precisely when grace shines in its finest hour.

Two principles were burned into my heart that I began
to live by after this event. First, in regard to my ex, anger
was always such an easy response. When recalling past
situations or dealing with new ones, I could and can easily
be filled with disdain. But I came to believe that, just like
myself and everyone else, she is simply another fallen soul
capable of making selfish decisions and creating devastating consequences—intentional or not.

As solo parents, if we put ourselves in the role of judge
and jury, we are continually tying ourselves to our ex and
his or her behavior. Our defensive actions look no different from their offensive actions. If we focus and funnel
our emotional and sometimes physical energy to attempt
to control life, we are diverting energy away from our children. We need our energy to build them up.

Choosing to bestow grace on an ex is a very difficult
choice, but it *is* a choice. In difficult divorces, it can be
easy to want to give ex-spouses "what is coming to them."
Instead, I had to make a conscious decision to surrender
my heart to my heavenly Father so He could help me
choose His way, not mine. Showing grace, even quietly
unspoken, actually frees us from the weight of our bur-

dens and, more importantly, is a critical example to our
kids. We *all* need grace—an unmerited gift from God—
and we must learn to express this on a regular basis, from
the most challenging of situations with our ex to our daily
interactions with strangers.

The Challenge and the Choice

Through this season and the keying event, I realized how
difficult it was for me to *accept* grace and to receive forgiveness. You, like me, may be guilty of some very destructive
choices. Maybe you are the one who left your spouse or
your entire family. The weight of shame and regret can be
just as crippling as the devastation of betrayal or abandonment. Regardless of what we've done or what has been
done to us, we all need to accept responsibility for our
actions while also accepting God's grace so we can move
forward in health.

SOLO CONFESSIONAL

"In 2010, my wife of thirty-three years left me—
and our five sons—for someone she met on
Facebook. Devastation and heartbreak hit us all in
the face. The abandonment and betrayal wreaked
havoc on our lives. Trying to make a living while
caring for the entire family alone was a one-day-
at-a-time, exhausting journey.

"While I was working hard to heal and
continuing to seek the Lord, in 2013 my ex-wife
escaped her second marriage, which had become

controlling and abusive. She had moved back to the city where I lived. Slowly, over time, we began to talk as I followed the path of forgiveness.

"We began spending more time together and even dating. In 2015, with all of our family by our side, and one son officiating, we were remarried, proving the eternal truth of Mark 10:27: 'All things are possible with God.'"

ROBIN

Not long after my encounter with God's grace given through Greg, I was having coffee with a very wise man, Al Andrews. Al leads an amazing organization committed to providing counseling to "creatives" in Nashville. I was telling him how ashamed I was about what had happened and how I didn't know if I could ever forgive myself, even though I was confident Greg and Toby had. Al listened with all the patience, empathy, and compassion imaginable and then quietly said something that completely changed the way I look at how God sees me. I will never—ever—forget his words.

Al looked me deep in the eyes and said, "Even though it is hard to get your head around this kind of grace, and even though it's hard to bring yourself to do it, sometimes the prodigal just needs to dance."

"What?!" I quickly fired back.

Al explained, "When the father saw his son off in the distance, he ran to him, threw his arms around him, and accepted him. Then he threw a huge party with the finest of everything. What we rarely talk about is what it must have felt like to be the prodigal. What's it like to know that you completely blew it in every way, that you committed the ultimate betrayal, that you made a total waste of time and resources, and yet the person you betrayed serves up a huge celebration to welcome you back?

"The prodigal has a choice—he can sit along the fringe of the party sulking, not accepting the honor bestowed on him, thinking *How can I dance with the weight of shame on me?*

"Or the prodigal son can decide to let go of the past and embrace the celebration. As shameful as he must have felt and how much he must have struggled with the idea, ultimately, he decided to dance at the party his father had thrown for him.

"The idea of not dancing at our own party—a party thrown for us—seems self-centered and ungrateful . . . so dance. Because we must celebrate our Father's love for us."

Al's words created a turning point for me. They were truth. I knew it and I felt it—maybe for the very first time.

We must accept this truth:

It is by grace you have been saved, through faith—and this is not from yourselves, it is the gift of God.

EPHESIANS 2:8

We can live in a humble spirit of celebration as the son or daughter who once was lost but has now come home. We have all been given a pardon—more than we deserve . . . "not by works, so that no one can boast" (Ephesians 2:9).

Front-Row Seat

In this unforeseen and unplanned adventure we have embarked on called solo parenting, God's grace must become the concrete we pour to build the foundation of our new normal. Our pain has placed us in a position to comprehend the depths of His charity.

We are *shown* grace to *show* grace. When we *show* grace, we *grow* in grace.

Whether we are fully responsible for what has happened to us or only an innocent victim, we must model grace for our children daily. Without this, our faith is empty. One thing I hope my kids learn from me is the principle of grace—both extended *and* accepted.

Putting grace into action in our lives requires applying a new daily filter on the way we see things—while teaching our children to do the same. Our worldview creates the way we live our lives, the spirit of our home, and the type of relationships we have—and will have.

When you are a solo parent, you have the perfect front-row seat to see and understand the ultimate manifestation of God's grace.

Accepting our own brokenness brings us to *receive* authentic grace.

Accepting others' brokenness brings us to *reciprocate* authentic grace.

6

MY ONE SAFE PLACE

My alarm went off every morning at 5:45. Now, depending on your frame of reference, that time may be ungodly early or horribly late. But I was a music executive, which is not necessarily a "morning person" career. Yet here I was, up with the sun, like it or not. Three little girls don't much care whether Daddy is an early riser or if he stayed up late working or paying bills. When they get up, guess what? You are up! My old normal had moved away, and no one had consulted me about the invasion of this new one.

In the middle of a typical night, Zara, my youngest daughter, would make her way downstairs and crawl into bed with me. Before I knew it, the alarm blast would summon me to get out of bed, brush my teeth, and brace

myself for the morning circus that daily paraded its three-
ring fun into the kitchen. All three girls were in school, so
the first hour awake required a lot of prep in a short window of time. Each day by 6:15-ish, I was acting as . . .

- Hair stylist (No, Daddy! That's not how the braid is
  supposed to look!)
- Caterer (Honey, be patient. I'm cooking breakfast
  while I'm making your lunch.)
- Fashion consultant (No, I mean it, babe. That dress
  still looks beautiful on you.)
- Drama coach (I'm sure your friend wasn't trying to be
  mean to you, and, by the way, we don't use that word.)
- Paramedic (No, Daddy, *I* have the hangnail. *Zoe* needs
  the Band-Aid for her knee.)
- Priest (Yes, before you all leave for school, we will pray
  for the hamster.)

Every day of getting those three ready and prepared for
school was fiercely familiar while mixed with a new adventure. Showers and hairstyles were one ordeal, while fashion choices were another. Finding out at the last possible
moment that the outfit carefully selected the night before
was now "awful" and could *not* possibly be seen in public
was challenging, to say the least.

Making lunches for school in the Beeson household
meant something quite different than the norm. My culi-
nary obsession made for more complicated preparations,
such as caprese salad with slices of tomatoes, fresh moz-
zarella, and basil, all drizzled with olive oil and balsamic

vinegar, stacked neatly in a mason jar. We prepared offerings such as Asian sesame noodles, pasta salads, or fresh wraps. I suppose thinking we just couldn't do the obligatory peanut butter and jelly made my mornings far more complicated. But making these meals also served as an important discipline. (More on this later.)

My children had the usual sibling arguments over who stole whose lunch box or hairbrush. After everyone was ready and had eaten breakfast we always prayed. The stop-everything-be-still-and-turn-the-day-over-to-God moment was critical to me, a priority even if something else had to be skipped. This is not because I am hyperspiritual, but because I was aware of how much all four of us needed God's help *every* day.

The first bus came around 6:30 a.m. and then the second at 7:45 a.m. In between the two departures, I would do my best to take a shower and gather myself for work. After Zara would catch the final bus, there were many days it took all I had not to crawl back into bed. It was always amazing to me how much of a mess could be made from their bathrooms to the kitchen to the front door in just a two-hour window! As you likely well know, the morning juggling act is always daunting when you're solo. And it's usually not if you will drop a ball or two, but how many?

Conflicting Compartments

As you likely also know, after the full-time job of morning parenting is done, a whole new life begins at the workplace. I was in the beginning stages of starting a new company from scratch. This second time was proving to be much harder for me, especially under my new circumstances.

My professional life felt very compartmentalized because of my stress at home. This, for me, created such a conflicting experience. Interacting with other adults while also worrying about my duties at home was a continual stressor.

While in the midst of an important project or crucial meeting, there was often a call from school with a distress message—Zoe forgot her lunch or Skyler wasn't feeling well. Whatever the call, it required immediate attention. In a heartbeat the day's priority would change, even though I needed to contact a studio to discuss the TV show's pre-production or my potential business partners or to download summer tour plans.

And then I needed time to deal with the legal side of child custody issues.

The girls' first bus would arrive home around 3 p.m., so I rushed to get as much accomplished in my workday as possible before meeting my girls at home. And being late when three little girls were coming home alone was never an option.

The late afternoon–early evening time was a mix of homework and business calls, coupled with questions and requests from the little beauties about what I thought about this or what I knew about that. And then, of course, there were the neighborhood friends coming over to play.

After some cleaning up from the morning, I would finish off business emails and head to my bedroom for fifteen minutes of alone time. There I meditated. I prayed. I was still. I reminded God of my need, and He reminded me of His love. I had to take time out to "Be still before the LORD and wait patiently for him" (Psalm 37:7).

When 5:50 p.m. rolled around, I started prepping for dinner, always doing my best to unplug from technology and be fully present with the girls. This did not come naturally for me, but it was considerably easier if my phone and laptop were left in the bedroom.

SOLO PARENT PRINCIPLE

When you have your children with you and you're attempting quality family time, leave your phone, tablet, and laptop in another room. If one of your children is old enough to have a cell phone or tablet, do the same with their technology too. You might regret missing an occasional call, but in the long run, this time will build relationships no one else or nothing else can replace. Others can wait. Your kids can't.

Cooking Up Community

I am convinced the kitchen is one of the most—if not *the* most—important rooms in the home to spend quantity *and* quality time as a solo parent. In Italy, the cities are peppered with piazzas—town centers where communities come together at night. I wish every city had these. They are places where true community is built. For our family, this interchange happened in the kitchen.

Here's how this worked. I would start cooking dinner.

Even if no one was in the kitchen when I began, inevitably, the girls would gather to watch me while natural conversations would begin about our days. No agendas; just authentic connections. This is where our fearsome foursome was most bonded and strengthened.

As a result, dinner became something sacred. This was far more than eating; this was experiencing real life. At least four times a week, we would sit around the table, always starting with prayer and then going wherever the conversation took us. Sometimes, a silly thing would become the focus. Other times, a heartfelt matter would rise to the top.

No matter what, these family gatherings around our table were always meaningful. And an incredible outcome of this time is that a cumulative effect begins to happen. The weeks, months, and years of this life intersection builds into a truly "unbroken circle." I cannot stress how important it is to set aside time for you and your kids to eat together.

The Bible speaks many times about this activity. Dining together satisfies our emotional and spiritual hunger as much as our physical appetites, if not more. Because the next morning, you *will* be hungry again, but your spirit can *still* be full.

There is a well-known Scripture about the integral elements that strengthened the early church:

> They devoted themselves to the apostles' teaching and to fellowship, to the breaking of bread and to prayer.
>
> ACTS 2:42

Note the third of the four activities listed. The writer differentiates fellowship from sharing meals. I think of the distinction this way: I might choose to hang out with someone at a coffee shop, but inviting the person to my home to sit at my table indicates a deeper level of relationship.

In fact, the four elements in this Scripture only grow in their intimacy—from public teaching to spending time in community to sharing a meal at the table to prayer with the Father. These four elements can be experienced inside our homes on any given night that we choose to take part in them, because in spite of the differences in age or roles, "where two or three gather in my name, there am I with them" (Matthew 18:20).

After dinner, as often as was possible, I continued our togetherness with some activity. In the summer, we often went swimming. We loved watching "nature shows," such as *Planet Earth* on BBC. I would always try to connect our faith as we would marvel at the amazing creativity of God. And personal technology was not a part of these times together.

After our activity, I made sure the girls' homework was completed, dishes were placed in the dishwasher, and the house was straightened up. Notice that I didn't say *cleaned* up. I will admit this detail usually had to wait for another time.

Inevitably, little spats arose at night between the girls. "Tell Zoe to get out of the bathroom!" "Skyler lost my brush!" "Zara wore my clothes without asking!" At bedtime, we said prayers, sprinkled with some discussion, and then the goal was getting everyone to bed and tucked in by

9:00 p.m. This could usually be accomplished if we started by 8:00. My days typically lasted about fifteen hours.

As a solo parent, you can appreciate my run-down of the typical day. While your details may be different, likely your overall schedule and struggle is much the same. The to-do list is endless. No matter the number of obligations, there are always more of them to do than we can get done.

Rest and Recovery

On most nights, by 9:30 the house was quiet. The chaos was over for a few hours before we would wake up and do it all over again.

During my solo years, fatigue was my dominating and ever-present condition. By the end of every day, I wanted *nothing* but quiet and rest. Not only my body, but my soul desperately needed a break. I relished these moments. Most nights, I probably should have gone straight to bed, but I rarely did because silence is such a rarity for us as solo parents. I knew if I lay down and fell asleep, the next thing I would face is the alarm reminding me it was once again time to get up and start all over again. I had to put some waking space between the last moment with the girls and the morning madness.

I would usually stay up for at least a couple of hours, just enjoying having no immediate demands on me and what I came to embrace as "me time." During these mini-sabbaticals I began writing, blogging, and mapping out this book. Sometimes I watched a Food Network show and fantasized about opening a restaurant. I would do anything that I didn't *have* to do. I worked hard never to take this time of the day for granted, while also attempting to come up with a few ideas of how to provide even more stability in my girls' lives.

A story is told of missionaries in the late 1800s who hired some local villagers to carry supplies through the jungle to a distant compound. The natives walked at a slower pace than the leaders. After the first two days, the main guide pushed everyone to go faster to cover more ground. The next day, the missionaries were pleased that they had covered twice as much territory. On the morning of the fourth day when the leader said it was time to continue, the native villagers stayed seated on the ground. After a few moments of ignored pleas, one of the tribesmen announced, "We went so quickly yesterday that we now have to wait for our souls to catch up with our bodies."

There is a level of exhaustion we come to live with as solo parents that a good night's sleep simply won't fix. We must commit time for "our souls to catch up with our bodies." Don't let guilt, drivenness, demands, or pride stop you from *real* rest for your soul. This always happened when I took time to practice the first of my Four Ps—Pause.

> Then God blessed the seventh day and made it holy, because on it he rested from all the work of creating that he had done.
>
> GENESIS 2:3

I *rest* my case. Pun intended.

Stranger in a Strange Land

One time while away on a trip, I was sitting in a Starbucks
in Marblehead, Massachusetts, writing. At the table across
from me was a woman pushing forty; her hair was pulled
back and she wore no wedding ring. She had been sitting
alone for at least forty-five minutes at a table for eight. She
stared ahead, lost in thought. Her face betrayed a sad but
humble resolve, a look that seemed to accept and say, "This
is my lot in life."

Behind her was a lively mixed group of men and women,
taking up every seat at their identical table for eight. They
were boisterous and full of life; their talk weaved in and
out of laughter and serious discussion as their hands boldly
expressed various points of view.

The solo lady didn't seem affected by them or the fact
that she was alone. There seemed to be an invisible barrier
between their table and hers. She was disconnected. I thought
her to be too exhausted to concern herself with their presence. I began to notice various expressions quickly sweeping
across her face. At first she seemed to be on the verge of tears,
then fatigued, and then apathetic. As she drifted between
those emotions, one thing was certain: She was completely
immersed in her own world. She was filled with solo
thoughts in a room full of community and energy.

Isn't it strange how so much activity can be whirling all
around us and yet anywhere, anytime, we can be contained
in a vacuum inside ourselves, lost in our own thoughts?

When you're solo, you can feel as if you're living in a
foreign country. It's disorienting, unfamiliar. It's not hostile,

but it definitely feels uncomfortable, as if you are an outsider. If you are to survive in a strange land, you must acclimate to new ways and customs. Observing that contrasting scene in the coffee shop reminded me of one of those quiet nights at home alone when I would reflect on life and try to create a strategy for a "new normal." I wanted to establish healthy habits, rituals, and routines—anything to build stability. Here are five habits that were significant for my family, as well as ideas from others on surviving in a strange land.

Habitual Habitation

As sinful people, we all have bad habits. It's just a matter of how many. I decided to focus on developing a few simple and new healthy habits that could help me reconnect to life and hopefully counteract the feeling of being so out of place and overwhelmed. This became the first step in developing the second principle of my four Ps—

Practices.

The first habit I adopted and put into action was revolutionary. MIT scientists have studied and proven its value to mankind as one of the most foundational forces in the universe. Are you ready for this first revelation?

Habit #1: Make Your Bed.

In his University of Texas at Austin's 2014 commencement speech, Naval Admiral William McRaven shared his ten life lessons from Navy SEAL training with the very first point being, "If you want to change the world, start off by making your bed. If you can't do the little things right, you will never do the big things right."

Let's be honest—it is easy to *not* make our bed, to just get on with our day as soon as we wake up, or get lost in the sheets and hide from the demands until the very last moment when everything becomes a hectic rush.

When I took a few minutes to make my bed, I was less tempted to crawl back in it. This made my room feel more like a sanctuary with more order and less chaos. Going to bed then felt more rewarding to turn back the covers to see the neatly tucked sheets. You know the feeling of peeling back tight linens and crawling in, as opposed to trying to find where one sheet starts and another ends from the wadded mess? This simple activity started my day off right by completing a "project" first thing in the morning.

> No discipline seems pleasant at the time, but painful. Later on, however, it produces a harvest of righteousness and peace for those who have been trained by it.
>
> HEBREWS 12:11

Habit #2: Start a Project You Can Complete.

We could call this one the "hobby habit." The simple goal and concept here is to just start something you know you can complete. Working out is a great choice for your physical health and stress relief. Gardening or planting flowers can be relaxing and rewarding. And as you have already gathered, my hobby was and still is cooking.

I could find a new recipe, gather all the ingredients, try it out, and serve the dish for dinner—killing two birds with one stone, as they say. Within an hour, I could begin a new, fun challenge and complete it all before evening family time.

When our world is consumed with so many loose ends and never-ending processes, when we're juggling so many details of life, it helps us to have something fun we can complete. I had never cooked as much as I did during my *solo* season. Playing chef gave me something to enjoy and a skill I could grow and develop. During that time, I studied recipes and constantly tried new ones. I watched cooking shows in any free time and then tried to duplicate what I saw—and sometimes I even attempted to improve the recipes. I experimented a lot—some recipes worked and some didn't—but most importantly, I accomplished my goal. Fortunately, my girls were always up for trying new dishes.

A new activity or hobby can . . .

- give you fresh focus,
- create satisfaction from a new accomplishment,
- offer productive free time,
- keep you out of trouble,
- keep you from falling back on old, unhealthy patterns,
- accomplish a secondary goal such as fixing dinner or getting in shape,

- become an avenue for meeting new friends, and
- defeat fear by trying new things.

Seek GOD, all you quietly disciplined people who live by GOD's justice. Seek GOD's right ways. Seek a quiet and disciplined life.

ZEPHANIAH 2:3, MSG

SOLO CONFESSIONAL

"The hardest part of being a single parent for me was the feeling of being totally alone. I enrolled in courses at the community college to give myself a purpose and have something to look forward to. It kept me centered and gave my mind something else to think about other than all my own 'junk.' For me, finding my strength in the Lord meant using the brain He gave me to figure out a better way to cope with all the emotions cascading over me during that period of time. A new venture and learning new things really helped me."

THOM

Habit #3: Create a Daily Touchpoint.

Reach out to at least one person *every* day. Don't wait on people to contact you. The Samson Society leaders encouraged each one of us to find a "Silas"—someone to check in with daily and "share the path with." My friend, Nate, who invited me to the meetings, became that person for me. I could call him anytime of the day or night for any reason.

Having a daily touchpoint helps keep us from drifting into dangerous isolation. My mom also provided me with daily interaction. We talked *every* day. I never felt as if I needed a reason to call or something specific to discuss.

This habit creates a physical reminder that we are not alone in this critical season. We are not meant to do life in isolation, so we must teach ourselves to not wait for others to reach out to us; we must reach out to them. For me, reaching out meant calling my mom each day as I drove home. Our conversations lasted anywhere from two minutes to more than an hour depending on what I was facing.

> Two are better than one, because they have a good return for their labor: If either of them falls down, one can help the other up. But pity anyone who falls and has no one to help them up. Also, if two lie down together, they will keep warm. But how can one keep warm alone? Though one may be overpowered, two can defend themselves. A cord of three strands is not quickly broken.
>
> ECCLESIASTES 4:9-12

Habit #4: Live Gratefully.

The habit of gratitude builds a unique strength in us. I once heard someone say that gratitude is gravity. In other words, gratitude is the force that attracts us toward something. I don't necessarily subscribe to the idea that thankfulness is a *natural* force that automatically affects us—at least it's not natural for me. But I do believe, especially in this solo season, we should do everything in our power to let gratitude keep us grounded. While this doesn't come naturally to us all the time, when life seems overwhelming, let the mind-set of thankfulness pull you back to a healthy place.

Let's face it. No one owes us anything, so we should be grateful for *anything* anyone does to acknowledge who we are, what we do, or what we might need. This worldview creates humility. We cannot entertain entitlement in any season of life, but most especially in the solo season. No matter how we got where we are, or what we face, we must train ourselves to search for things that we are grateful for, no matter how small.

> Give thanks in all circumstances; for this is God's will for you in Christ Jesus.
>
> I THESSALONIANS 5:18

Habit #5: Engage in Prayer and Meditation.

Whether I felt like it or not, and often I didn't, I learned to set aside dedicated time to quiet my mind and be still. This became one of the most important facets of my new normal.

Now depending on your spiritual or denominational paradigm, you may have come to believe meditation is a non-Christian activity, but, in reality, God created this first. As is so often the case, the enemy has robbed us and reidentified a Christian paradigm as his own. Meditation is simply a focused discipline to usher *you* out and usher

God's presence in. This state of mind then opens us up to intimate prayer with the Father.

Sara Lazar, a Harvard neuroscientist, found that meditation creates important physical changes in your mind by increasing brain density in areas responsible for self-control, focus, problem solving, flexibility, and resilience. Best of all, these changes become permanent.[1]

I knew this had to become a habit for me because there were days prayer and meditation didn't feel important or I thought I didn't need it as much, which meant I could at some point easily stop altogether. But each day that I committed to this discipline, I felt centered, present, and stress wasn't so great an issue. I had to push pause on life just long enough to take some deep, cleansing breaths, quiet my mind, and remind myself that God would meet me there in the space I cleared away only for Him.

When we set aside time for God, He can embrace, recharge, strengthen, and restore a sound mind within us. I learned that the Christian life is not just about victory and overcoming, but surrender and letting God provide and protect. I find I more easily trust God and His ways when I quiet my mind and listen to Him.

Get your minds ready for good use. Keep awake. Set your hope now and forever on the loving-favor to be given you when Jesus Christ comes again.

1 PETER 1:13, NLV

> ## SOLO CONFESSIONAL
>
> "Anytime I hear a worship song today, I am always reminded of the joy I found in the midst of the heartache of divorce when I spent time praising the Lord. It shifted my focus from the pain of the situation and helped me to see Jesus more clearly. My ex-husband held me down, but Jesus always lifted me up. I was so tired and beaten down, but worship allowed me to feel free again."
>
> TAMALA

These habits might sound simple and perhaps a bit mundane to you. Or maybe you are thinking, *I don't need one more thing on my plate.*

But here's the point of cultivating these habits: When you do, your commitment to your personal growth sets a valuable tone for your overall outlook on a new life. I encourage you to seek out not only these, but also your own new habits to counteract the constant feeling of chaos as you are solo.

Here are some habits other solo parents have found helpful:

- "Several months after my wife died, I joined a boxing gym. This became a huge stress relief. I lost weight I had previously gained, plus an additional ten more pounds. The exercise helped improve my attitude, and the gym gave me a chance to start meeting new people and become more social."

- "Loading (or unloading) the dishwasher and starting a load of laundry first thing in the morning seemed to jump-start my day. When I do these things, my day is productive. When I don't do these early in the day, it is harder for me to find my momentum and I don't get as much done. Figure out what sets the tone for you, and make that part of your daily routine."

- "When the kids interrupt me as I am doing laundry or yard work, my first instinct is to address their immediate concern and then send them away with instructions to entertain themselves until I am done. I have learned that it is more beneficial to the kids (and usually to me) if I invite them to join me. I say something like, 'I will look at your [latest cool thing] when I am done with laundry. But if you will help me, then I will be done faster.' Typically they will help because they want my attention. This gives us an opportunity to simply coexist, and they share things with me as we work that they would not ordinarily talk about."

- "Team work! Tackle big or unsavory chores as a family. No one in my household is keen on keeping up with the lawn, so we do it together. One child picks up sticks and toys while I am on the riding mower and the other child does the trimming. For laundry, one person runs towels to the linen closet while the other two fold as quickly as possible. One child handles the clothes that need to go on hangers while the other takes care of those that go in drawers."

• "Prepare for the next day before bed! Our bedtime routine includes setting out clothes for the morning, getting backpacks ready, packing lunch bags, and laying out morning meds. Doing this ensures that little to no clear thinking is necessary while we are all still half asleep in the morning."

Redemption and Restoration

Have you ever remodeled a house? If you have, you will definitely understand the difference between redemption and restoration.

When you purchased the house, you made a transaction; you paid for it. That's redemption: "the action of regaining or gaining possession of something in exchange for payment or clearing a debt."[2] Redemption is *transactional*.

When you began ripping up carpets and refinishing the house's wood floors, you began the restoration. Restoration is "the action of returning something to a former owner, place or condition."[3] It's a process that is often slow—at times, painfully slow. Yet restoration is more than transactional; it's *transformational*.

As you face your solo season, it's important to understand the difference between God's redemption of your life and His restoration of your life. For a long time, I didn't understand these concepts in spiritual terms.

I grew up in a fractured home, and that raised questions in my mind. I had heard all my life about how God redeems. But if God redeems, why was our family still broken? Why couldn't things be put back together? When my parents split, I felt so alone. Even though I knew God was with me, I wondered why that fact wasn't enough to make me feel whole. I felt lost most of the time even though I was supposedly found.

Understanding the dramatic difference between redemption and restoration was a major breakthrough for me. We can be redeemed yet not restored. We can be saved and still feel broken. Being broken is not something that needs fixing. I came to understand that embracing broken-ness and confessing my dependency are not weaknesses at all, but actually a gift from God.

We were created for need. Need is how we feel loved by God and others. Without need, there cannot be provi-sion. Without being broken, there can be no restoration. In fact, you cannot restore what *isn't* broken. So accept-ing brokenness as an ongoing state of need is actually freeing.

On all those TV home-makeover shows, if the family "drops by" to see the house when the rooms are gutted and the walls are torn out, they might be surprised by how it looks but they don't panic. Why? Because they know resto-ration is in process and what they are seeing must occur for the final result to be experienced. Workers strip the rooms down to the framing. The house looks nothing like what it was before. But even the way it originally looked was better than it looks now. Yet when the work is completed, the homeowners will quickly forget the few days when their house was just a shell. That's restoration—taking every-thing down to the essentials and building something beau-

tiful that can be far better than the original. *Both* beautiful
and better.

There is a good chance you feel like you are stripped
down to just the frame of your former self. But I promise,
a Master Builder sees beyond the way your life looks now
and He is in the process of building something beautiful
and better.

In this home-makeover analogy, someone must first
gain possession of the home by paying the price. *That* is
redemption. Redemption is always the first step of restoration. But to improve the condition, a builder must
carefully . . .

1. Strip out the old.
2. Remove the damaged parts from the home.
3. Make significant improvements.
4. Create new and lasting value.

I used these four steps in my own life to assure myself
that restoration was actually happening. To do this, I first
accurately acknowledged my circumstances when only my
"frame" remained. I encourage you to honestly and accurately assess your state right now.

Next, surrender to God, confessing Him as the only One
capable of redeeming and restoring you and your family.

Lastly, focus on the end goal—the intent of the Builder—
to turn this mess into something beautiful. For thousands of
years, God has been in the business of redeeming and restoring people. He was more than able to do that for my girls
and me, so He can and will for you and your family as well.

Once I was finally able to come to grips each day
with the concept of restoration, I felt the one-thousand-
pound weight strapped to my shoulders lifted from me.
Acknowledging that my life was stripped down to the
frame was expected for what had happened, normal for
where I was at this stage, and important for me to accept.
I didn't need to frantically try to "fix" *anything* right now.
This state helped me begin to sense some sanity and peace.
But it's crucial to remember the first step in restoration is
not just the demolition, nor the actual building, but the
planning.

In a few episodes of those TV home-makeover shows,
the homeowner has to live with the home "as is" for a while.
This happens because the most critical part of restoration is
taking place—establishing the vision, dreams, and plans for
what this home can be and will be. Work cannot start until
a master plan is in place.

During the planning process, we see the walls and rooms
only as they *are*. But a builder sees what *will* be. The builder
is not limited in scope as the owners are. The builder believes
if the foundation is stable, then virtually and visually *anything* is possible. Knock out a wall here. Build a wall there.
Put windows where solid walls are. Move fixtures. What once
was a bedroom can now become a bathroom. What once was
a large bonus room can now become a master suite.

While our own home was under construction, I would
go to the work site almost daily to view the progress. There
were days those signs were hard to find. In fact, what was
being built often looked very different from my copy of
the plans. A little too often I would question how what I

was seeing would ever turn into what was on paper. A few times, I even became skeptical of the builder, asking things like, "Is this cabinet really six feet? Looks like four to me." "This hallway looks way more narrow than the measurements on the plan." Construction was an often frustrating and far too lengthy process. But in the end, I had to trust the builder and the plans we had agreed upon. I had to trust that what he envisioned to be built, what he saw up on top of that hill, would match the plans.

The only time I felt relief from frustration and impatience was when I spent time with our builder, Rick. He assured me that everything was on course and he was happy with the progress.

"We'll get it right," he told me constantly.

In times of restoration, we are often disheartened and impatient—partly because we can't see how our lives as they are now can be turned into something beautiful, especially after all the destruction in our homes. Often, we really don't know what we even envisioned a restoration would look like. I certainly couldn't tell what I wanted at the time. I just knew I didn't want to build what I had before. I knew couples who seemed to have successful marriages, but in those times, I didn't trust that I was capable of having a happy marriage.

The problem comes when we ask for the wrong thing or don't even know what to ask for. When I started planning for the construction of our house, I had to spend time with the builder. I had to think through what was important to us in a home. I was fortunate to be able to take part in designing our plans. Had I just copied what everyone else

was building, we wouldn't have ended up with a home that
we felt was perfect for us. If I hadn't worked with the right
builder, I wouldn't have had the opportunity to see what
was even possible.

> Trust GOD from the bottom of your heart; don't
> try to figure out everything on your own. Listen for
> GOD's voice in everything you do, everywhere you
> go; he's the one who will keep you on track. Don't
> assume that you know it all.
>
> PROVERBS 3:5-6, MSG

God is our Builder. Slowly with time and healing, like the
Good Father that He is, new life will begin to be revealed
when He holds the plans. And for you and your children,
while your home is being restored in this solo season,
He always offers a permanent residence in your one safe
place—His love.

> The Lord is my rock, and my safe place, and the
> One Who takes me out of trouble. My God is my
> rock, in Whom I am safe. He is my safe-covering,
> my saving strength, and my strong tower.
>
> PSALM 18:2, NLV

7

A FIRM PLACE TO STAND

IN THE MUSIC BUSINESS, success is as much or more about the convergence of timing, resources, and relationships as it is about creativity and talent. Releasing an artist's project is about finding the optimal window in the market for the music to get maximum attention and momentum. Therefore, the production, packaging, marketing, and assets have to be completed well in advance.

Ever heard of "bingo fuel"? Well, I certainly never had.

At a committee meeting for our record label, one of the other executives had returned from an event where an astronaut had been one of the keynote speakers. The aeronautical expert had explained the concept of bingo fuel as the point in the mission where there is just enough fuel to return safely to Earth. At bingo fuel, the spacecraft must end its mission and begin its return trip home. In other words, this was the space program's way to identify the level of fuel prior to reaching the absolute point of no return—literally.

So in our company, we started using this term as a way to identify the drop-dead final deadline for a recording while still optimizing the album's release. Being the strange mix of procrastinator and perfectionist that I am, I used this phrase a lot. I would often ask my staff what the bingo-fuel point was for an album—the latest possible date I could turn in the master recording and still get the project out in our release window, while firing on all cylinders in every department.

But in the summer of 2006, bingo fuel took on a different and deeply personal meaning for me. I had done the math: When my bank account level reached a certain dollar amount, I would no longer be able to pay the mortgage and maintain our lifestyle.

I had certainly brought everything in the budget down to as modest a level as possible. I found our bottom line, as the accountants say. If we crossed that bingo fuel number, I would have to give up on starting another company and find a "regular job." My days as an entrepreneur would be over. We would then have to sell the house and most likely move from the area, probably into a small apartment, which would mean a change of schools along with many other challenges for the girls.

I had been meeting with investors for months, trying to find funding for my new company. I had literally exhausted my entire list of potential partners. Many had shown great interest, but had also now, one by one, taken a pass on getting involved.

The panic kept me up at night. I was constantly pacing the room trying to figure a way to make this dream a reality. While I knew I couldn't do it on my own, I seemed to be convinced there had to be an angle I hadn't seen or a stone I had yet to turn over. And I so hate feeling helpless. It is one thing to know bingo fuel is just ahead, but knowing you cannot change your trajectory is quite another.

My friend Troy had told me about an out-of-state group that might be interested in investing, but they were a long shot. This group wasn't familiar with the entertainment industry. Regardless, this looked like my last chance. The odds of them investing in me, someone they had never met, were slim. But I was only weeks away from my bingo fuel so I set up a meeting.

Staring at my fuel gauge pointing dangerously close to the "E" on the command center of my life, I decided to prepare my girls for what I feared was about to happen.

Promise on a Porsche

At about 2:00 one afternoon, I called all three into the living room. Kids know you are serious when they are all summoned together. They sat on the couch with a mix of curiosity and dread in their eyes. I jumped right in.

"Girls, you know I have been doing everything I can to keep us in this house, to keep life as unchanged as possible.

You also know that I've been trying to find partners to help start this new company. I believe God is completely in control and nothing that is happening is a surprise to Him. I believe we've been doing our best to be wise with our money. I don't have all the answers to the many questions about the future, but I wanted to let you girls know where we are now . . .

"We're running low on money, and although I have been trying to find people to help fund this new company, I haven't yet. There is one other possibility, but I want to be honest with you. If this doesn't come through, we may have to make some big changes . . . and we might have to move. I have tried to avoid this, but sometimes things just happen. And I don't want you to be surprised if this happens to us."

I paused, bracing myself. But they were completely unmoved. They gave me the quintessential kid's look of "So Dad, is that it?"

Zoe spoke up, "I'm not worried. As long as we're together, we could live under a bridge." And with that declaration of family unity, we moved on to another subject.

Ten years later, I asked Skyler, my middle daughter, what she had thought at the time about that situation. She responded, "I was never worried because you had always told us that God would take care of us, and in every situation up to that point, He had."

Right after our bingo-fuel discussion, we went on one of the girls' favorite and free outings—visiting the animals in the pet store at the mall. As we arrived and pulled into a parking spot, Zoe pointed out something that was written on the window of a Porsche Cayenne in white marker. The words read, "Those whom God has placed their foot upon a rock, shall not be moved."

This was one of the most blatant ways that God had ever spoken to me. It was a profound moment. As we all looked at the message scrawled on the luxury car's window, Zoe stated, "Dad, I think God is trying to tell you something."

So I thought, *What* are *the chances of us pulling into a spot in a crowded mall parking lot, right next to an $80,000 car with a 'God message' written on the window?* This, right after our family had just talked about the inevitability of running out of all available options visible to *me*.

"Those whom God has placed their foot upon a rock, shall not be moved."

Psalm 40:2 exploded into reality for me that day. "He lifted me out of the slimy pit, out of the mud and mire; he set my feet on a rock and gave me a firm place to stand."

My Foundation, my Rock, was my God, not my bank account. God was my Source, not a list of investors. God would save us, not a big check. In desperate times, it is so easy for us to make the wrong things into saviors.

While the end of bingo fuel may be a cruel death sentence for an astronaut crew, this position is actually the best place for a believer to be. This is the place where you can grasp the provision of a very real God. Living at the edge of no return is good. Most often, we don't find death there at all, but real life—and God's grace.

Personal Provider

The Bible is filled with bingo-fuel moments. One of the most clear and close calls was the story of Abraham and Isaac. Just as their gauge hit a no-turning-back level, God brought the answer.

> Some time later God tested Abraham. He said to him, "Abraham!" "Here I am," he replied. Then God said, "Take your son, your only son, whom you love— Isaac—and go to the region of Moriah. Sacrifice him there as a burnt offering on a mountain I will show you."
>
> Early the next morning Abraham got up and loaded his donkey. He took with him two of his servants and his son Isaac. When he had cut enough wood for the burnt offering, he set out for the place God had told him about. On the third day Abraham looked up and saw the place in the distance. He said to his servants, "Stay here with the donkey while I and the boy go over there. We will worship and then we will come back to you."
>
> Abraham took the wood for the burnt offering and placed it on his son Isaac, and he himself carried the fire and the knife. As the two of them went on together, Isaac spoke up and said to his father Abraham, "Father?" "Yes, my son?" Abraham replied. "The fire and wood are here," Isaac said, "but where is the lamb for the burnt offering?" Abraham answered, "God himself will provide the lamb for the burnt

offering, my son." And the two of them went on together.

When they reached the place God had told him about, Abraham built an altar there and arranged the wood on it. He bound his son Isaac and laid him on the altar, on top of the wood. Then he reached out his hand and took the knife to slay his son. But the angel of the Lord called out to him from heaven, "Abraham! Abraham!" "Here I am," he replied. "Do not lay a hand on the boy," he said. "Do not do anything to him. Now I know that you fear God, because you have not withheld from me your son, your only son."

Abraham looked up and there in a thicket he saw a ram caught by its horns. He went over and took the ram and sacrificed it as a burnt offering instead of his son. So Abraham called that place The Lord Will Provide. And to this day it is said, "On the mountain of the Lord it will be provided."

The angel of the Lord called to Abraham from heaven a second time and said, "I swear by myself, declares the Lord, that because you have done this and have not withheld your son, your only son, I will surely bless you and make your descendants as numerous as the stars in the sky and as the sand on the seashore. Your descendants will take possession of the cities of their enemies, and through your offspring all nations on earth will be blessed, because you have obeyed me."

GENESIS 22:1-18

Abraham didn't bring the ram with him. He didn't devise a Plan B. He didn't have a visible option. God spoke and sent the offering at the perfect time. But as Abraham was walking up that mountain, so was the ram. Not in sight, but the plan was in motion, unseen and unknown, until Abraham was right at bingo fuel.

Staring at the message on that Porsche's window in the mall parking lot, I surrendered my circumstances too. I decided that the God who provided a way for Abraham—the God who promises to lift me out of the slimy pit, set my feet on a rock, and give me a firm place to stand—is *my* Provider and my *girls'* Provider. No matter what happened next, He still would be our Provider. And here's the great news for you—He is *your* Provider too!

Two weeks after our mountaintop mall moment, the investors I had never met before miraculously funded the business. Suddenly we had money in the bank to start a new company and stay in our home. I learned a lot about faith from my kids' reactions *and* Zoe's statements ("I'm not worried, Dad. God is trying to tell you something."). And I learned a lot about provision from *the* Provider.

The word *providence* comes from the Latin word *providential* and means, essentially, foresight or making provision beforehand.

So unbeknownst to me, before my bingo-fuel moment was even close at hand, God was being "provident" and making provision in advance from people in another state I had never met.

I would imagine you have either been in this position of desperation or are at that place now. You may even be

staring at the big "E" on your fuel gauge. You have raised
the "knife" on something in your own life, just as I had
on our home and all that we knew. But I hope that by
hearing my "Porsche promise" experience and one of the
Bible's most well-known stories, you can come to know
that God's provision is just as real as your bingo-fuel
reality.

The Abraham and Isaac passage is the first time the
Bible describes God using the name "Jehovah-jireh," which
means Jehovah God, my Provider. *My Provider.*

I had always associated that name with God meeting our
needs of shelter, food, and essentials. While our Jehovah-
jireh can certainly take care of the basics, I learned that He
can do so much more. During my solo season, I encountered what I believe Abraham was saying—that God was
the One who provides the way through the most dire of
circumstances.

This experience also positively affected my relationship with the girls. When I chose to be open with them,
to humbly acknowledge the problem facing us and
confess I didn't have an answer, our bond grew deeper.
And the fact that they were unfazed because I previously had spent much time pointing out the faithfulness
of God in every way possible was a reaping of what I
had sown.

While we can privately thank God when He comes
through for us, I believe making those moments into foundational cornerstones in our families is important. Taking
time out to celebrate when God moves in *your* family—
no matter how big or small the situation might be—is

so valuable. The Israelites built altars to commemorate God's faithfulness. We need those markers in our homes to remind us He does His most powerful work when we run out of visible and viable options.

I realize this can be difficult, especially for those who have lost a spouse to death. I asked a widow friend how her family focused on remembering the faithfulness of God when it would be easy to argue that He wasn't faithful. I found her answer inspiring: "We try to find things to be thankful for and remind ourselves there are always worse things people are going through."

There are many ways to celebrate God's faithfulness and provision as a family. Here are ideas from other solo parents:

- "Simply thank God out loud for things, saying things that God obviously sent us—whatever they may be. Acknowledge the blessing so my kids see that it is a blessing that God sent and learn how to be thankful for it."

- "We actually collect stones—Ebenezer stones—and hang plaques to remember God's faithfulness. I try to constantly remind and celebrate with the kids that they have two loving parents."

Harvard psychologist Dr. Chirban says, "We must become our child's compass to impart direction, to point towards truth. We don't have to have all the answers but we need to lead the way."[1]

SOLO PARENT PRINCIPLE

Be creative in developing ways to connect your faith to the reality of what God does in your family. Learn to acknowledge with your children when He moves and works. This can be as simple as thanking Him with them when He does answer prayers. This deliberate focus on gratitude and spiritual connection will help them build their own "firm place to stand."

Relationships, Routines, and Rituals

The bingo-fuel situation also made it clear that I had been missing a key parenting role. I learned that there is a difference between being a provider and an establisher. Let me explain.

During my solo season, I worked hard to keep the many plates spinning in the air. Paying bills, buying groceries, cooking, housework, homework—all needed to get done. But my ability "to get it done" also is how I measured my care for the girls. Just as in Abraham's case, God wanted to do more than simply provide a means to an end. He wanted to establish a quality in our characters that would become virtually immovable. I needed to start looking beyond simply providing for needs. I needed to begin establishing the ladies that my girls were going to become. Along with the deliberate habits I had started creating in our home, I needed to be intentional about how we lived our daily lives. Building rituals and routines is an important facet of the second of my four Ps: Practices.

What were Abraham and Isaac sent to Mount Moriah to do? They were to build an altar and sacrifice to God. They were to perform a ritual. According to the *Oxford Dictionary*, *ritual* is defined as "a religious or solemn ceremony, consisting of a series of actions performed according to a prescribed order." I believe there is something to the discipline of rituals. As proactive parents, we must work hard to establish character in our children. Developing who they will *become* is of equal importance to what they need *now*.

The word "ritual" often has a negative connotation in our culture, but in reality we practice rituals every day. Consider how you start your mornings. Chances are you have a precise order regarding what you do after you climb out of bed. Brushing your teeth, jumping in the shower, making a cup of coffee, catching the news, praying and reading—these are all rituals, and rituals are important. They give preparation and organization to our days, and they are as unique and different as our signatures. Rituals also are crucial to families.

A ritual I remember quite vividly growing up happened every Wednesday. My dad and I would get up early and go to McDonald's for breakfast. Today, I cherish those memories. When I was a boy, my mom would always come in my room and pray with me. We'd also sing "Children of the Heavenly Father" together. I hold both of these regular rituals with my parents close to my heart to this day. Some might simply call these routines, but I choose to see those times as being far more significant and worthwhile than a routine.

My parents created rituals: regular, intimate, and intentional connections that I could count on. Simple as they were, they meant more than the action taken as my parents set aside time to honor and value me.

During this season of unpredictability, our kids crave stability—things they can count on.

Rituals don't have to be made into a huge deal—they just need to be consistent with the intent of honoring our kids.

SOLO PARENT PRINCIPLE

What rituals might you create with your children? Consider their unique personalities, interests, and needs in your decision. The key is personal, quality, and undivided time given on a regular and predictable basis to deepen your relationship and bond.

Likely because I have such vivid memories of my family's rituals and what they meant to me, I started looking for simple things I could do to create positive moments and memories for my three girls.

Every Sunday evening after dinner, I would take them into my room with a basin of warm water, some fragrant soap, and a soft towel. They would sit around me and, one by one, I would wash their little feet. I have always loved the practice of foot washing in the Maundy Thursday services during Holy Week at church. I would take my time, focusing on one daughter at a time. After I gently rubbed the soap and warm water over her feet, I would dry each foot, and, finally, say a short blessing over her. Doing this for each one of my daughters was my way of saying, "I may be your dad and the head of this house, but right now, I am humbling myself to show you I am here to serve you and express how important you are to me."

I hope those moments and the intentional humility and service will stay with my girls the rest of their lives. Regardless, this was a good practice for me. It helped me to not only focus on providing for my children's basic needs, but also on establishing a sense of significance for each one.

Jesus first modeled this ritual as a way of expressing love and commitment to His disciples. He knew that the significance of His physical service to them would soon be a very special memory for each one.

> Jesus knew that the Father had put all things under his power, and that he had come from God and was returning to God; so he got up from the meal, took off his outer clothing, and wrapped a towel around his waist. After that, he poured water into a basin and began to wash his disciples' feet, drying them with the towel that was wrapped around him. He came to Simon Peter, who said to him, "Lord, are you going to wash my feet?" Jesus replied, "You do not realize now what I am doing, but later you will understand."
>
> JOHN 13:3-7

The one ritual the global church has continued since its inception was encouraged by Christ Himself, so we would realize His great love and sacrifice for us.

When the hour came, Jesus and his apostles reclined at the table. And he said to them, "I have eagerly desired to eat this Passover with you before I suffer. For I tell you, I will not eat it again until it finds fulfillment in the kingdom of God." After taking the cup, he gave thanks and said, "Take this and divide it among you. For I tell you I will not drink again from the fruit of the vine until the kingdom of God comes." And he took bread, gave thanks and broke it, and gave it to them, saying, "This is my body given for you; do this in remembrance of me." In the same way, after the supper he took the cup, saying, "This cup is the new covenant in my blood, which is poured out for you."

LUKE 22:14-20

"Do this in remembrance of me" is an invitation to take part in a ritual of faith among all believers.

In our family, simple rituals were equally important, such as making certain I wrote a quick note for each girl and put it in her lunch box for school. The notes were never long or detailed. They could be as simple as "Zara, remember that I love you today." I would often draw a simple stick figure of Zara and I together, which would always make her laugh because I am a terrible artist. Or I would write, "Zoe, I am so proud of you and happy I get to be your dad! Have a great day!" The point was just reminding the girls that I was thinking about them.

And, of course, there was one important ritual I discussed earlier—sitting down and eating dinner together as a family. During mealtimes, I deliberately tried to direct attention and conversation to things we were grateful for. There is huge strength in maintaining gratitude in our families. I also saw the importance of scheduling individual one-on-one "daddy dates" with each of them, making sure they all knew they were equally cherished for their uniqueness.

Then there were the silly rituals.

No mom in the house and having all girls proved to be challenging in the area of female beautification. I admit I was out of my league. So I made the best of it by creating a character to celebrate the process. Enter Jean Marco (pronounced Zhahn). I'm not sure exactly where this character came from—maybe from watching extreme hairdressers' commercials. My slight Tennessee drawl would transform into a French accent and flamboyant mannerisms as I highlighted and styled their hair with pomp and panache. My girls were either very brave or my Jean Marco character was quite convincing. I suspect it was their bravery, coupled with the fact that they really had no choice. But they do say French accents are commanding. *Oui, oui!*

My father was an amazing provider, even in the most difficult of times. But what I remember most were the times he listened to, played with, and was completely available to me *and* for me. In every dependent relationship, there is the need to provide. This is not a bad quality, but I suppose in its simplest form, I am saying that no amount of money or provision can substitute for our primary, primal responsibility to build into and establish the adults our kids are going to *become*, and, hopefully, the strong disciples of Christ into which they will *transform*.

Media Magnets

As I spent so much time at home with the girls, I began to realize the amount of media my now "tween" girls consumed. Statistics tell us the average tween spends an average of six hours a day absorbing various media, which represents some forty to forty-five hours per week.[2] That is literally a full-time job! In fact, tweens spend more time there than anywhere else in their lives—eating, sleeping, school, and certainly far more than they spend in church or spiritual activities. As a solo parent, I often found myself turning on the Disney Channel and letting the TV entertain my girls while I caught up on life. The truth is that it's easy to make media the babysitter-on-demand when we feel we have nothing to give or feel other activities must come first.

SOLO PARENT PRINCIPLE

While the chances of eliminating all of your children's screen time are virtually impossible these days, consider where and when you can create limits. Think about "screen-free zones" in your schedule when devices are not in use. Reading is a great form of education and entertainment that can be introduced to your children. Consider allowing an hour of screen time followed by an hour of reading in the evening.

Another fact ringing in my ears and convicting my spirit at that stage was George Barna's research declaring that "what you believe by the time you are thirteen is what you will die believing."[3] Another report I read stated that 43 percent of people who accepted Jesus Christ as their Savior made the decision before their thirteenth birthday, and 64 percent made that commitment to Christ before age eighteen.[4] Quite frankly, these facts added pressure to my job as a parent.

This was one of the most critical seasons my girls would ever face. This time in their lives was determining the core of their identities for the rest of their days, and it terrified me. But this realization was also the genesis for what would become the greatest work of my career.

When I considered the fact that "tweens" devour massive amounts of media every week, just when so much of their identities are being formed, I took a closer look at what was available in the market. I realized that there was no Christian media company creating biblically based entertainment for this age group. There really were no choices for a Christian parent that would also be accepted by and attractive to their preteen kids.

At this point, I was in the process of starting a new Christian media company. With this new conviction, however, I decided to put all of my focus and efforts into launching an entertainment company exclusively for "tweens." My house with my three girls could be R & D— the research and development department—for this new endeavor. Together, maybe we could reach into the lives of millions of "tweens" around the world and let them know they are more than what the world's media is telling them to be. They are loved, designed with a purpose, completely unique, and valued by the Father who created them.

It took me forty years to learn the truth about my identity in Christ, and now I wanted to commit my life to letting these precious kids know this truth much sooner than I did. Maybe if we could get to them before the age of thirteen, their foundation, identity, and roots would be so strong and deep that what the world throws at them in the teen years and beyond would have far less impact. This could be one of the big-picture reasons why I found myself alone with my girls in this season of life. As Max Lucado states in his interpretation of Genesis 50:20, "In God's hands, intended evil becomes eventual good."[5]

Life Imitating Art

So I started my new—and current—media company, iShine, in my living room with my girls. People now liken us to a faith-based Disney—minus the theme parks, of course. We have a TV show, teen music artists, CDs, DVDs, books, Bibles, web community, and national touring events. Today, iShine is the largest Christian "tween" media company in the world. And this dream started in the middle of my solo season. When everything else was stripped away, my life's work was revealed.

My daughters were not only the inspiration for the creation of the company, but also my partners. While building this business was certainly hard work, we were able to have a lot of fun together. In the early days they were with me constantly—on the set of the TV show, acting in some of the episodes, on the tour bus, and sitting with me in the casting auditions for talent. Creating this company united us and helped turn the dark times into a mission of hope.

The "i" in *iShine* stands for identity and is by far the most important issue facing our modern times. We need to learn and accept who we are, or better said, *whose* we are. During this season, I was beginning to answer that question for myself, and I wanted so much for my girls and kids everywhere to discover the truth before their worldview was locked in for the rest of their lives. After all, media *is* the doorway to this generation. They're already watching and listening, so why not use the language of media to communicate Christ's message?

I learned early in my music career that if you want to influence someone you first need to find out *what influences them.* While the concept sounds simple, it is sometimes counterintuitive. If we have something we want to get across, we are often quick to just say it without being aware of how the message is being perceived. Yet if we want to predict how a message will be received, we need to know a lot about *who* is about to receive it. This concept applies in any relationship. Influence starts with listening, watching, and getting to know those you want to affect, whether they be children, tweens, coworkers, or a nation.

I told every artist as we got ready to record an album, "Always choose connection over expression." Having an important lesson or point of view is one thing, but if we don't have an effective way to communicate that message, to connect with people, so often our valuable point is lost in the method we use to deliver it. So rather than simply and quickly expressing the message, first seek to connect and to understand the audience. Don't assume they will "get it."

In parenting, there is another way to communicate this truth: Method is everything. We need to weigh carefully *how* we deliver our message as much as *what* the message is.

I remember getting ready for work one morning and thinking how I needed the girls to take on more babysitting jobs. I also wanted them to ask for "sponsorship" from family and friends to help with the enormous cost of extra-curricular activities such as cheer and dance.

Yeah, I thought. *This will teach them responsibility as well as help bear the load a bit.*

We have a home intercom system that allows me to push a button and talk to the girls in their rooms. I decided I would get my thought out right away by using the inter-com. But right before pushing the button and suggesting to my girls that they should make a babysitting flyer and write fund-raising letters for sponsorship, I caught myself.

Really? Was I actually going to lay this burden on them over the intercom, just like I was asking them to pick up their room or telling them it was bath time?

I stopped myself and took a bit of my own medicine, thinking, *How I deliver this message will strongly contribute to how it will be received.* So I changed methods and had a constructive, sit-down, face-to-face, "we can do this" con-versation.

Not everything requires a formal meeting, but I would

venture to say that in those days, more often than not
I tended to just bark out words that fell on deaf ears.
But with the right method and connection, I could find
receptive hearts. It helps to express encouragement, moti-
vation, kindness, patience, and gentleness with the message. Ask "How will they *hear* it?" before "How should
I *say* it?"

It is so important to take time to listen and understand
where our kids are, *who* they are, and how they are influ-
enced. This is the first step to guiding them and the most
important step in building authentic relationships.

The Orbiting Oddity

Focused and intentional parenting can have a dark side.
One of the biggest mistakes I ever made with my girls happened during this season.

A few years into my solo journey, I noticed it was easy
to become so consumed with what was going on in my
kids' lives that I started to lose perspective on healthy
boundaries.

I felt so badly about the things my girls were going
through and what they had already experienced that I tried
to overcompensate by making them the center of my universe. I would quickly drop whatever I was doing to take
care of their needs or desires. I didn't want *anything* to disrupt them or make them uncomfortable.

Here's the best way I can explain my mind-set at that
time: I began to orbit their lives. Healthy families have the
parents in the middle, as the center of this microuniverse,

with the kids orbiting them. These parents set the rules, beliefs, and vision that then create the gravity to keep their kids safe, secure, and grounded.

Divorced parents—even with all the good intentions in the world—often have a tendency to put the kids in the center of their universe and let their kids' needs become the gravity. This is dangerous. God intended for us, with Christ as the Core, to be the parent and leader, with the kids as the followers. In Ephesians 5:23 Paul says that Christ is the head of the church; in our families, parents should represent Christ and the kids the church. If this principle is inverted, the home's stability is threatened. Our kids need a firm foundation. The proper biblical model for a home has always been the parent in the center, strong and consistent, unmoved by the gravity of life in its orbit. This is the natural *and* supernatural order. For stability and consistency to exist and everyone to be healthy, our kids cannot be the center of our universe.

In a recent interview for the Solo Parent Society podcast, I spoke about this topic with Sissy Goff, MEd, LPC-MHSP, and director of child and adolescent counseling at Daystar Counseling Ministries in Nashville. She explained that orbiting your child's universe can create emotional entitlement in your kids. When a single parent, with all good intentions, constantly shields his or her children from discomfort or overcompensates to help them avoid pain, kids can start to believe this is how the world works, Sissy said.

Children end up thinking this way: *My parents did everything to isolate me from pain. So now, anyone who comes into my life must do the same thing. It is their job to make me happy.*

Over her twenty-four years of counseling, Sissy said she has seen danger in this trend of emotional entitlement. "You are doing your children a disservice and, in a way, crippling them because they become entitled and demanding, which isn't healthy for any future relationships or even how they see the world," she explained.

Once I realized I had succumbed to this dynamic, undoing the chaos took more time than I would have liked. To discourage the emotional entitlement mind-set, I needed to take care of myself first. I had to take time to recharge and process my life with others. I would have to differentiate between my girls' absolute needs and nonessential desires. But creating new habits has never been easy to do. First, I had to again let go of my codependency, let go of somehow believing that I was able to fix all the problems and hurts my girls faced. I couldn't play god to my girls.

Secondly, I needed to trust that the *real* God was fully capable of caring for them and healing our home. Making sure my girls were happy all of the time could not be my goal. I couldn't—and shouldn't—try to remove the shadow of death, the hard things my girls faced. I just needed to be with them as they passed through the valley. I was and am not "the firm place" on which my girls must learn to stand—Christ is.

8
FINDING TRUE NORTH

She was by far the prettiest barista at the local Starbucks that I frequented, a beautiful brunette with deep blue eyes. Bekka was an aspiring singer-songwriter (imagine that in Nashville?) making ends meet by creating an amazing sugar-free-vanilla-Americano-with-an-extra-shot-and-nonfat-milk drink. I had certainly noticed her during my everyday fancy fix of caffeine but hadn't paid too much attention until this much younger woman struck up a non-coffee conversation with me one morning.

"Do I know you from somewhere?" she asked, taking me by surprise.

I thought for a moment and then answered, "I don't think so." I smiled and quipped, "Other than being here almost every day."

"Well, you look like someone who's in the music indus-try," she guessed.

Frankly, I didn't care what her motive was. A beautiful young woman was choosing to make conversation with me for the first time in a very long time . . . and it felt great.

As it turns out, Bekka was, as they say, an old soul with incredible taste in music. She made a practice of forsaking the chart toppers and the current flavor-of-the-week artists for the likes of Joni Mitchell; Crosby, Stills, & Nash; and other classic 60s and 70s legends. Our common interest and her touch of musical rebellion created an immediate connection.

Over the next few months, we spent many hours in conversation developing her music. I am confident that deep down I was doing my best to charm her in an attempt to undo the damage my divorce had inflicted on my ego.

Because many of my friends were women, spending time with Bekka wasn't that unusual to anyone who knew me. But this relationship was different—and cathartic. We had no history. She didn't know my ex-wife and the details of my past life. She didn't know me "back then" and was completely outside my usual circle of close friends. And the proverbial icing on the cake was that Bekka found me attractive despite what I had come to believe about myself. Vain or not, this brought fresh hope to my heart.

Before we met, I didn't understand how deep my need for companionship actually was, but this relationship began reopening a curiosity toward the opposite sex that had been dormant for years.

Might there be another woman out there for me? Dare

I think about that as a real possibility? Was I ready to go beyond the friend zone and reenter the world of romance? The impossible was starting to feel, well, not *so* impossible.

Unfortunately, there is a tough barrier to break through on the way to new love—particularly for *Christian* solo parents—and that's allowing ourselves to be attracted to others.

For thirteen years of marriage, I had programmed myself to not even *look* at other women, much less entertain the idea of starting a relationship. I was married. I was committed. To change that programming, even after divorce, is no easy task. Looking at other women and thinking *What if?* just did not feel appropriate, even a few years after the divorce.

So how do you "deprogram" yourself and begin to consider a future with someone else? And, more importantly, when do you open the door to dating again after divorce? I can confidently confess now that there is no absolute answer to the *when* question for any of us. It is a very personal decision.

The "Starting Over" Lie

First, I firmly believe the idea of "beginning again" is a myth, if not an outright lie, for the solo parent. There is no such thing as *starting over* with children in our care. Believing we can wipe the slate clean or step up to a brand-new starting line is a trap. Our lives are already in motion and are not going to stop. We just don't have the luxury of suddenly acting independently, of thinking life is just about us and our happiness. In fact, that thinking usually results in poor choices that hurt solo parents' children. Don't get me wrong. I like starting new things. That's how I am wired.

But I knew I couldn't have a "fresh start" with Bekka. To consider starting over with someone that young was about as impractical and fantastical as believing I could compete in the next Olympics!

Eventually, I had to face the reality that the gap in our ages and life experiences trumped any attraction or desire for a soul mate. The train of life that the girls and I were on was not only moving quickly, but it was way down the tracks from this young woman. Entertaining the thought that somehow we could start a new life together would be setting my family up for fatally false expectations. I needed to connect with someone whose train was already traveling the same direction and speed.

While Bekka and I never referred to our friendship as dating, we had both realized the companionship we experienced might be meeting immediate needs, but not long-term ones. Age, interests, personal history, places in life, future goals, spiritual priorities, and many other factors helped me face the falsehood and infatuation of the "starting over" lie. I am fully convinced that this belief is a major reason the divorce rate in second marriages is 17 percent higher than in first marriages.

If you are reading this book, I'm going to bet your own train is already on the tracks and barreling through the countryside. You are not at all certain where your train is going, but you know you are moving on down the line! As you speed ahead and begin to envision a future mate, you'll want to avoid three traps that I've learned can derail you and your family.

Trap 1: Rationalizing your motives

Jeremiah 17:9 says, "The heart is deceitful above all things and beyond cure. Who can understand it?" We all know we can rationalize any decision. And every decision is driven by our motives. When we begin to talk ourselves into something that we know is selfish or not at all the right thing for our children, we are in trouble in every area of life. Learn to check yourself when you begin to go down Rationalize Road and figure out where the nearest off-ramp is located. As a solo friend of mine says, "*No one* is ready to be in a relationship until they are comfortable being single. They must feel whole by themselves before there can be a healthy romantic/partnered relationship."

Trap 2: Romanticizing your journey

Both genders are often guilty of putting on rose-colored glasses when attraction or romance enters the picture. We lose a sense of reality and begin to paint a picture of our lives that is not possible or healthy. To be clear, I am not talking about having goals or dreams for an incredible mate. I'm talking about having unrealistic and dangerously selfish aspirations for a relationship. Romance is a necessary quality for a healthy marriage, but romanticizing our potential new life in an unhealthy manner can lead to a dangerous liaison. Often, people say that they aren't ready for a relationship but that they are dating casually. They are simply having dinner and hanging out, they'll say, but they know they have wounds that need healing before they develop a relationship. This approach can be dangerous, because relationships *will* develop. Feelings will emerge—in you or the people you date—despite your best intentions. Those feelings may be ones of endearment, which threaten your resolve to avoid a relationship before you are emotionally ready. Or they may be feelings of rejection, which can deepen your wounds and increase the time it takes to become emotionally healthy and stable.

Trap 3: Reprioritizing your children's lives

As solo parents, we naturally circle the wagons around our kids early on, as we should. But when we begin to entertain a new relationship, rationalizing and romanticizing can lead to changes in those proper priorities, and we may place ourselves or the new person before our children. The care of our children is job one from day one in this new life. And this must be our calling until they leave us for their own lives. Sacrificing our needs is tough—it's a delicate balance between knowing our kids' *needs* versus their *preferences.*

One solo mom put it this way:

> My children, having watched their father move on immediately after moving out, were confused about why I wasn't dating. My own conclusion was that I was in a fairly healthy place but that I didn't have a *need* to start dating. I had not worked out for myself

what I would seek in a romantic relationship, what I would accept, and what I would not accept.

I was just beginning to think about these things when I met John. My lack of preparation for dating meant that the start of our relationship was a bit tricky. Was I making decisions that were truly in the best interest of myself and my kids? Or was I relying too much on my own feelings? Thankfully, John was understanding and encouraged me to put my kids before him. The lesson in this is that dating requires preparation. I would encourage others not to begin dating until they have worked out boundaries for themselves. A few things I would have liked to work out for myself in advance were the importance of faith in a relationship, if I would consider a long-distance relationship, the parameters and boundaries for sexual activity, and questions about money/ education/station in life.

As you begin to entertain the idea of a new relationship, keep these three traps in mind. If I had decided to force-fit Bekka into my life, as well as the girls' lives—even if she had been willing—I would have encountered each trap, and my girls would have suffered the consequences. We must decide for our kids' sakes to avoid these traps and keep our train on the tracks. You still can be hopeful. You can be expectant. You can change and grow. But be *realistic* about your past and present so you can be *reasonable* about your future.

> ## SOLO PARENT PRINCIPLE
>
> Before you begin to think about dating again, it is crucial to take a self-assessment. Ask yourself these questions: *Where am I in the healing process? How would my dating affect my children?* This is not so much about having the right answers but getting a clear picture of where you are and how a change will affect your kids.

For any of us, the following Scripture tells the best and only true way any brand-new start ever happens:

> When someone becomes a Christian, he becomes a brand new person inside. He is not the same anymore. A new life has begun!
>
> 2 CORINTHIANS 5:17, TLB

"A new life" applies to God's work in us. Don't shortcut or avoid the process that God has started in this season, most especially the work He is doing in you, your children, and your family as it is right now.

This acquired revelation of truth kept me from entering the dating world for several years. I decided to focus intentionally on healing, especially in the area of relationships. If I were ever to have another soul mate, I would first have to get a grasp on my own life and work on being ready to bring someone else into my world, while entering theirs in the *right* way. This included gaining a correct and healthy perspective on what I was even looking for in a mate. But I knew I couldn't do that until I addressed my own unhealthy patterns.

SOLO CONFESSIONAL

"For me, dating in the solo season began with honesty. As a Christian, I came to the place where I felt I was doing the right thing before God. Then I was honest with my children. I avoided confusion by making sure a date never filled the parent role. I introduced them to my children as my friend. After all, they should be my friend, right? This approach was much easier on the kids if and when things became more serious."

BILL

To Love and Be Loved

My deep desire for companionship or the ache for human connection to love and be loved *never* went away. God Himself has placed that desire in us all, so while it can hurt for a season when we are alone, the fact that we have the desire is ultimately good. When I would feel that need rising up in me, I did my best to submerge myself in worship so I would be reminded of the true source of love in my life.

While this practice never eliminated my desire for a physical person and presence in my life, receiving the love and grace of my Father did overcome the immediate need to fill that physical ache. Holding someone's hand, being held, or looking deep into another's eyes—and everything that comes along with that—are primary needs that I am not diminishing by suggesting you just turn on some moving music. Yet if these needs are not kept in the right context, they can actually extend our time of restoration because we keep placing temporary physical Band-Aids on our very real and quite large emotional and spiritual wounds.

We must constantly remind ourselves that the Spirit of God is just as real as any need we have. He is able to move in our lives beyond words or human expression, even in a way we can physically feel. Choosing to reflect on His work in our souls can soothe and comfort us far beyond our ability to even articulate the hurt and pain. This verse in Isaiah was meaningful to me during my solo years:

> Your Maker is your husband—the LORD Almighty is his name—the Holy One of Israel is your Redeemer; he is called the God of all the earth.
>
> ISAIAH 54:5

And I love these words from Wesley's hymn "Jesus, Lover of My Soul":

> *Other refuge have I none*
> *Hangs my helpless soul on Thee*
> *Leave, ah! Leave me not alone*
> *Still support and comfort me*
> *All my trust on Thee is stayed*
> *All my help from Thee I bring*
> *Cover my defenseless head*
> *With the shadow of Thy wing*

While I recognized my needs and desires, I began to believe that God's love for me was very real, with Him being, as Isaiah says, my "husband." That was enough for me in this solo season. If one day God chose to bring someone else into my life, it would be His idea and would simply come out of the overflow in my relationship with Him.

Creating Community

God had placed several close female friends in my life who supported me during this time. Jordyn and Nina were colleagues at the record label where I worked. We had all been friends even outside of the office for more than ten years. They were extremely helpful with the girls, becoming like surrogate mother figures in their lives. We would spend holidays together, share meals regularly, and even go on trips together.

Jordyn and Nina were a godsend to the girls and me in my solo season. They cared deeply for my daughters as their own—and still do. Their strong and confident femininity reaffirmed and supported my young women and helped guide them in the ways only estrogen can when I was incapable of providing or sometimes even understanding the right solution. Jordyn and Nina stepped into our lives and assumed crucial roles for which I was not at all prepared or wired.

God also will send others to help you. He can create a community of His making. He will provide what you and your children need. I didn't say *what* you want *when* you want it, but what you *need* when it is *time*. This is why your prayers and obedience are so vital in your parenting.

Be sure you seek out all the opportunities available to you, such as church, small groups, or support groups. I know sometimes single parents feel awkward walking alone into church with kids. You may feel as if everyone is looking at you to either judge you or figure out your story. I can assure you that while this sometimes might be the case, most of the time your concern is probably due to a heightened sense of insecurity.

So many single parents I have interviewed for the Solo Parent Society podcast or Solo Parent Society groups have stressed how significant and important being plugged into a community was in their healing process.

Our children need strong, gender-specific role models to confide in and emulate. I was fortunate to have two of my closest friends step up and fill that gap. Consider what Matthew says:

> Whoever welcomes one such child in my name welcomes me.
>
> MATTHEW 18:5

> Which of you, if your son asks for bread, will give him a stone? Or if he asks for a fish, will give him a snake? If you, then, though you are evil, know how to give good gifts to your children, how much more will your Father in heaven give good gifts to those who ask him!
>
> MATTHEW 7:9-11

I didn't have to ask Jordyn and Nina to "welcome" my "little children" into their love and care. They just did. And God, in His great mercy and grace, gave these two women to my three girls as His "good gifts." He answered my unspoken prayers of *Help!* with His helpers. I can tell you with all confidence that God will provide the right people—His people—to bless you and your children in this solo season. To repeat and personalize: How much more will your heavenly Father give good gifts to [you] who ask Him.

For those of you who did the math, you may have questioned why God only sent two women to my rescue when I have three daughters. Enter Chelsea.

I first met her when she was an intern at Camp Hopetown. She took an immediate interest in my girls and connected with them. In fact, everyone at Daystar Counseling Ministries, which conducts the camp, surrounded them with wisdom, acceptance, and love. But Chelsea zeroed in on my daughters individually and made herself available anytime for whatever they might need.

Chelsea is one of the wisest young women I have ever met. Sometimes I reached out to her, and other times she contacted me to check on the girls. I could share any of my concerns about any of my daughters with her. She would respond by taking that one out to get ice cream and talk. She made herself available and present at just the right times. And so the girls had someone who unconditionally reached out *to* them and processed life *with* them.

Identifying gender-specific people who will be good mentors and role models for our children is important. Solo parents need help, and we cannot be afraid to ask for it. And when God sends assistance, take it! I understand how difficult it can be to reach out or even accept someone's help. I once felt that if I accepted support, I would be admitting failure. But every time I swallowed my pride and said "Yes," the enthusiastic response I received was so reassuring and healing. The emotional lift I felt when I accepted someone's offer was an added bonus.

The truth is, we all become like the people who surround us. We resemble those we associate with. We conform ourselves to the community we create. We create the community to which we conform.

Faults, Fear, and the Future

Over the years, I had spent much time reflecting on all that I had contributed to the demise of my marriage. A few years after the divorce was final, I noticed something had changed. This process was no longer a shameful exercise. Somehow, it was freeing.

I had come face-to-face with the reality that in my marriage I had been

- controlling,
- distant,
- self-absorbed,
- driven (to an unhealthy point),
- good at fostering close relationships *outside* of my family,

- less and less dependent on relationships *within* my family,
- an enabler,
- afraid of intimacy, and
- a self-contained father and husband.

When I say self-contained, I mean I ran from the feeling of needing anything or anybody. I was doing my best not to be affected by any outside influence so I would never get hurt. While it seemed like a good plan at the time, I was setting myself up for both a failure and a fall.

When I look at that list of glaring shortcomings, I see that all are rooted in one overarching factor: Fear, with a capital *F*. Fear that if I didn't have control of situations or people, I would somehow come undone or be exposed. The truth about me would be found out. While the triggers vary, every single parent has to battle fear.

A growing relationship with our Father helps us to understand that fear

- breeds negative beliefs,
- brandishes bad attitudes,
- builds unhealthy attributes,
- becomes a lousy motivator,
- blindfolds our faith, and
- binds us from the life God intends.

A healthy exercise would be to work through this list and specify any negative beliefs or bad attitudes that you have developed or that may be creeping into your life. Any

negativity from your divorce and/or the trauma you have
experienced can breed fear, which then creates unhealthy
attitudes. Dealing with these now can bring healing and
diminish your fears.

I would read 1 John 4:18, "perfect love drives out
fear," and then wonder how the verse is supposed to look
in everyday life. How do I walk that out? I had a hard
enough time undoing the destructive habits that had
already contributed to my failed relationship, let alone
building a better life that anchors itself on love without fear.

One day I was having coffee with my friend Heidi and
she was sharing about her dating life. She had started seeing
a divorced man whose first wife had accused him of being
too controlling. But now he was compliant on *everything*.
He wouldn't make a decision. His new role in a relationship was being a doormat. He was using Heidi to prove he
wasn't controlling.

During this conversation, I realized we cannot simply
"fix" our past shortcomings by acting in an opposite manner. If we are simply altering behaviors without changing
our hearts, we won't move forward. Our goal should be to
improve our character, not disprove the negative aspects of
our past.

When we can fully realize the love we have in and
through Jesus, we can then believe that any shortcoming
is actually a pathway to freedom *from* fear. This freedom
can relieve us from having to control situations in an
attempt not to get hurt. We can start to believe in a very
real way that our Father is trustworthy, and He does have

everything in control for our benefit. Remember this verse:

> "I know the plans I have for you," declares the LORD, "plans to prosper you and not to harm you, plans to give you hope and a future."
>
> JEREMIAH 29:11

Through all of the relationships that deepened or developed in my solo season, from Bekka, Jordyn, and Nina, to Chelsea and so many others, and after years of processing all of the faults and feelings I've shared thus far, I started to believe I was actually capable of sharing my life with someone. I was coming to terms with God saying it was "not good for [me] to be alone" and accepting His future plan. I sensed a readiness to allow myself to hope—to hope that it is possible to have a healthy relationship and build an even better future.

SOLO CONFESSIONAL

"While I feel I've done a good bit of healing and moving forward in the last seven years, I have realized that all I know about having a husband is what the first one did to me. I find some days that I almost expect the reactions of my current husband to be the same as my first husband's. But it has been somewhat strange to feel like I can just be exactly who I am, and my new husband loves me just for me. I have not known that before."

KIM

Becoming Somebody's "Right One"

So let's go back to the question we posed at the beginning of this chapter: How do you begin to find the "right one" when you are already a life in motion, already a "train on the tracks"? How do you even know what you are looking for?

I defined the quest as finding my true north. A compass doesn't work until you establish where you are on the earth's axis. Without that important bearing, the directional instrument is not reliable. So finding true north becomes the first priority if you are to travel to a destination.

The right *direction* is more important than the right *path*. If you know *where* you are heading, you will begin to see multiple *ways* to get there.

However, if there is no direction, then the focus must become completely about the path. A life with no direction is unpredictable and dangerous.

I slowly began to realize that I needed to stop measuring others according to my great expectations and instead allow God to help me become the person He desired me to be. What good is it for me to expect God to bring along "the right one" if I wasn't willing to become someone else's "right one" first?

To illustrate this point for middle school and high school boys, a friend of mine asks them to write down the qualities of the woman they one day want to marry. Ninety-five percent of them give him the profile of a supermodel with the intellect of a brain surgeon and the personality of Cinderella. Then he asks them this question: "What kind of man are you going to have to become to attract a woman like this?" This is always a sobering moment for the teenage brain.

After I focused on becoming who God wanted me to be, God would have to send someone my way. The woman would need to be headed in the same life direction as my girls and me, committed to the same values.

When I discovered this new perspective, I grew excited about my future. You don't look forward to a trip until you know the destination, right?

I was no longer trying to undo or fix the old habits but rather focused on God's love for me and allowing His transformation. This approach freed me from my old standards of measuring relationships.

Over coffee with a friend one morning, I was sharing my excitement about finding someone traveling my direction when he said, "That's great—so what are you going to do about it?"

I had no answer.

"Robert, as long as I have known you, if you wanted something, you just did it," he said. "You built a company. You signed artists. You sold millions of records. So, what are you going to do about *this*?"

Honestly, that question was deflating. I didn't go to bars. I knew I didn't want to find love at Starbucks. Or the grocery store. Or the mall. And at church, most everyone was already part of a family. You don't want your place of worship to become about finding a mate.

But I couldn't believe what he asked next: "What about eharmony?"

I immediately wanted him to keep his voice down. How embarrassing! Internet dating? I think not, sir!

"Tell you what," he said. "Try it. If it doesn't work in ninety days, I will pay for it. What have you got to lose?"

So, soon after that conversation, reluctantly, as if I were admitting failure at meeting someone the "normal way," I started filling out the digital pages and viewing personality profiles. I wasn't expecting it to be so in-depth.

I also wasn't expecting to meet Barbara.

9
LIKE A CITY ON A HILL

As I HESITANTLY BECAME an eharmony patron, and after sifting through many names and profiles, I discovered a lady named Barbara. Following the rules and protocols for everyone's protection, we talked online before eventually sharing phone numbers. The conversations became more frequent and continued for several months. But there came a point where we both knew it was time to meet.

The day of our first face-to-face date finally came. Our ministry team was on the final day of shooting the *iShine* TV series. At the end of every episode, I talk to the camera for two minutes. In those segments, I try to cast vision and share what we hope to be the outcome for every episode, encouraging parents and kids to talk openly and honestly together about the topics we address that they are facing.

On this particular day, the shoot was taking longer than usual, probably because my attention was elsewhere. I kept thinking, *What if her online photos are ten years old? What if she notices my own photos aren't that current? What if she discovers that the angle of my profile shot was intentional to make me look ten pounds lighter? What if my receding hairline causes the sweat on my dome to glisten, drawing her eyes more to the hair I don't have than the hair I still have left?* You see where this was going, right? Totally irrational paranoia had set in. Sheer fear. Although I probably wouldn't have admitted it at the time, I was officially freaking out.

When we were done with filming, I called Barbara. We had been planning this first official date for a couple of weeks. After a very long, intense day, I was exhausted. I don't know if it was nerves or being so tired or both, but I suggested we meet up another evening. Although we had become quite comfortable talking, this meeting felt overwhelming—in an excitingly terrifying way— like when the roller coaster you weren't sure you should ride is heading slowly up the first hill. You have committed to the ride, so just pull the seat belt tight and hang on.

To Barbara's credit and courage, she came right back with, "Uh, I think we have waited long enough." And the date had already been postponed once before. I actually loved and respected how honest and forthright she was.

This relationship was going so well on the phone and

online that part of me was worried: *Would meeting in person just mess up a good thing? Was I being like an artist who rehearsed and rehearsed the show but never got on stage?* At some point, you have to risk the next step.

Allowing for Overflow

Barbara was right (a pattern I would soon find to be consistent). I agreed with her and we set the time and place.

In mid-February, the chill of winter was still hanging on to Tennessee. I arrived early at one of my favorite restaurants and waited for her at the door. Ironically, this was the same place where I drank too much before vandalizing TobyMac's promo van. Hopefully, this night would go far better than that one did. As I waited, I wondered if I would recognize her from the online pictures.

There was no mistaking her as she walked up. She was wearing an off-white sweater, a tweed skirt, and boots, with a scarf tying the entire ensemble together. Curls of beautiful strawberry-blonde hair framed her porcelain face. She was gorgeous! Therefore, a quick, panicked thought swept over me: *Maybe if I ran around the building a couple of times, I could drop a quick ten pounds.*

But my fears were put to rest as we officially introduced ourselves, face-to-face for the first time. I wondered what to do as I met her. Shake hands? Kiss on the cheek? Awkward hug? Fist bump? We opted for the hug, which was not at all awkward, and then the hostess showed us to our table.

The conversation seemed a bit forced at first. When you get to know someone online or on the phone and then suddenly you are right in front of the person, your mind wants to default and start from the beginning again. After all, this is the first time you've *really* met.

Yet the truth is that countless hours of heart-to-heart communication develops a deep understanding of the other person. Like a collision of the senses, the emotional and spiritual knowledge of the person now merges with physical attraction. After all, the age-old phrase is "love at first *sight*." The eyes finally connect with the person whom the heart has already engaged. At least in my case, it didn't take long for all my senses to catch up and get on the same page now that Barbara was sitting across the table from me.

We talked for hours after dinner, closing the restaurant down. This became the new norm for months to come. When we went out, we would end up being the last people in the place, learning to ignore the people stacking chairs and mopping floors. We just kept talking, deepening our connection. I had so many thoughts and feelings bottled up that I felt as if Barb had popped the cork on my heart. My words couldn't stop flowing. Being completely transparent and fully known—without the encroachment of fear or insecurity—to a beautiful woman who had also been parenting alone in her own solo season was amazing for me.

On one of our early dates, Barb casually interjected a tough question, asking if I had ever had a moral failure in my prior marriage. Without hesitation, I answered yes, and then began confiding to her what had happened in those early years. As my story poured out, I was a bit shocked at myself. In the past, I would have reserved that conversation for much later in a relationship—if I ever chose to share it at all. But here I was, opening up in a new way.

My solo season had obviously dismantled my need to pretend to be something I am not. The truth was, and is, that I am a broken man. I have made many mistakes. Now I lived daily in a confident state that I am held together solely by the grace that is much larger than me, or anything I had to offer. I didn't want any relationship in my life to involve pretense or deception. I had lived the separate roles of father, executive, "creative," boyfriend, son, brother, leader, and Christ-follower, but for the first time all of those roles were fully integrated into one holistic person with a singular identity. This was a new but welcome change for me. The change came only after I surrendered all I thought I was and accepted one simple truth: It's not who I am, but *whose* I am that defines me.

My identity was secure in Jesus Christ, and all that I was, I am, and will be flows out of that sole position as a child of God. By connecting my heart to Barb's, I was able to see and confirm the work that God had done in me. In His redemption, He had not only healed me, but also readied me to share my life once again in His way.

I have been crucified with Christ. My ego is no longer central. It is no longer important that I appear righteous before you or have your good opinion, and I am no longer driven to impress God. Christ lives in me. The life you see me

> living is not "mine," but it is lived by faith in
> the Son of God, who loved me and gave himself
> for me. I am not going to go back on that.
> GALATIANS 2:20, MSG

With this new mind-set as my baseline, I was no longer afraid of being known completely and letting Jesus take me wherever He wanted me in my business, relationships, and every circle of life.

A Current Event

Many years before the demise of my marriage, I was in Paris and spent one day alone walking the city, lunching at a tiny bistro, intentionally getting lost, and ultimately sitting on the bank of the Seine River. I was completely content and happy to not fit in anywhere for a day. I was okay with not knowing my way around and being surrounded by unfamiliar sights and sounds. As I sat and watched the steady flow of the river, its water illustrated a life lesson for me.

Two pieces of wood were drifting along. One thin, long twig, which looked freshly cut, was being moved rapidly by the current and appeared to just skim across the surface. The other piece of wood was shorter, thicker, and obviously aged; it was waterlogged and creeping along, half submerged.

I could have seen these two pieces of wood in any river anywhere, but I saw them at this moment, in this city. Maybe it was just the effect of Paris, but I felt as though God was trying to tell me something.

At that time in my life, I was on a fast track running my music label, which was experiencing tremendous growth. I was at the "top of my game," as they say, but also detached from just about everything. What occurred to me was that even though life was fast, furious, and exciting, I was actually, in the frenzy, missing out on life itself. I was moving too quickly to actually take anything in or let anything soak in. I was living but missing the essence of life. I was traveling at high speed at an altitude of 30,000 feet, completely oblivious to the ebb and flow below. And something needed to change.

Even though the small twig was moving through the water quickly, it was absorbing nothing, never slowing down. I imagined this branch was focused completely on getting somewhere as fast as it could with minimal impedance. I realized this: Life isn't rich if you don't slow down and absorb it. Speed might get you somewhere faster, but that's not what this journey of life is all about.

The more weathered and worn you are, like the second piece of wood, the more life lessons you can absorb, the more you become part of the flow, and the more in tune with the current you become.

God allows us to constantly grow, change, experience, and absorb the lessons of life. But the best approach that promises growth is slow. We may often rush through life because we want to avoid pain. If we work hard to stay on the water's surface, we miss what the river has to offer by not becoming a part of the flow.

This was a lesson for me in contentment, satisfaction,

and peace. I was not supposed to fight what life brings my way, but trust that I will move with the current as God wants me to within whatever season I find myself. I can take in as much of the journey as possible, becoming richer for being slower.

This is exactly why the season of being solo is so important. The process of moving from hurting to healing is slow, but God has much to teach us during this time. Remember, either the season defines us or we define the season. Either we choose to move through the pain of divorce or being solo as quickly as possible, or we choose to surrender to the current and God's pace of restoration. I stopped fighting the time in between "what was" and "what was going to be" and started paying attention to the story God was writing in my life that very moment.

The Four Ps

The primary lessons I learned during my solo season can be divided into what I call my *Four Power Principles (Four Ps)*.

- The Power of Pause
- The Power of Practices
- The Power of Perspective
- The Power of Prayer

1. The Power of Pause

As I have emphasized previously, meditation and prayer served as my pause.

To pause means to

- take a break in a pattern, to suspend an activity temporarily;
- disengage from what is consuming our attention, even if for a few short moments;
- quiet our mind from all the noise of the world and allow God to remind us of what is real, that He is with us and for us; and
- deliberately stop what we are doing to restore our strength.

For this principle to work, you must intentionally plan pauses during your regular, daily schedule.

> Be still before the LORD and wait patiently for him.
> PSALM 37:7

2. The Power of Practices

When you put into practice positive, healthy routines and habits, you establish a sound foundation for rebuilding your life and your children's lives.

To harness the power of practices:

- create simple routines that establish patterns you and your children can depend on;
- initiate rituals that celebrate your family;
- schedule time for authentic connection with your children—for example, planned meal times; and
- remind your children of their identity and how loved they are via notes, phone calls, or texts.

Finally, brothers and sisters, whatever is true, whatever
is noble, whatever is right, whatever is pure, whatever
is lovely, whatever is admirable—if anything is
excellent or praiseworthy—think about such things.
Whatever you have learned or received or heard from
me, or seen in me—put it into practice. And the God
of peace will be with you.

PHILIPPIANS 4:8-9

3. The Power of Perspective

This principle starts as a discipline—something you need
to consciously practice—but can and should eventually
become a default thought pattern. After I began dating
Barb, I realized how much my perspective had been permanently changed. Unlike before, I now trusted that God was
completely in control. I could truly be myself and stop role-
playing based on who was in the room with me. This new
perspective became my fail-safe setting for my identity.

To change our perspective, we must accept the simple
principle that if we look for God in the situation, we will find
Him. In fact, I will go so far as to say we will *always* find what
we are seeking. If we look for things to be frustrated about,
we will find them. If we look for things to be thankful for, we
will find them. What makes the difference? Perspective.

But there is a deeper issue here that shapes everything.
Let me give an example.

About a year before my wife left, she and the girls were
at Disney as I was returning home from a business trip.
I came home around 10:00 p.m. to an empty house. The
quiet, especially after a whirlwind trip, was welcomed.

All the rooms were dark except for a couple of lights I had turned on. Suddenly, the silence was pierced with a faint but distinct cell phone ring. Two rings, in fact, and it wasn't my cell phone. My heart skipped a beat, and my chest tightened.

We lived in a two-story home on a cul-de-sac at the top of a good-sized hill that was surrounded by trees and fairly isolated from traffic and streetlights. I grabbed a flashlight and slowly started checking the downstairs rooms. I tried to quell the thoughts of an intruder being in the house.

My search produced nothing, so I turned on almost every light downstairs in the house and went into the kitchen to make a quick dinner. Not five minutes into making a plate of pasta, I heard the two rings again. But this time it sounded louder and closer. I grabbed my keys, bolted for the door, got in my car, and called the police.

I told the person at 911, "There is someone in my house!" Calmly, she stated, "Okay, sir, stay on the line until officers get there. They are already en route."

Within three minutes of my call, two police cars pulled up with lights and sirens on full display. After I explained what had happened, the officers told me to stay put. I gladly obliged as they hurried into the house.

About five minutes later, they signaled for me and disclosed that they had searched every room, under every bed, in every closet, and didn't find anything. Another officer returned from walking the perimeter of the house with the same report. Nothing.

Embarrassed that I had created drama for the local police, I started making small talk. They were very gracious. But just as they were saying their obligatory "If anything else comes up, don't hesitate to call," the cell phone rang again. But this time, they heard it too. Guns drawn, the police officers ran upstairs toward the sound. Now feeling vindicated, I braced for gunshots or at least the sound of shouting and a scuffle . . . but there was nothing.

Just then, one of the officers called from upstairs, "Mr. Beeson!"

"Yes," I yelled back.

"Well, it appears Barbie has been trying to reach you."

The girls had not turned off one of their Barbie cell phones lying in an upstairs closet. Now I was the laughingstock of the Franklin Police Department. I am quite confident that the "Beeson and Barbie Case" is still archived as one of the most ridiculous but amusing calls they have ever received. I could just see one of those guys at a law enforcement conference saying, "Oh man, that's nothing! Listen to this one."

Join the ridicule if you want, but when that cell phone rang in that large, dark, empty house, it was easy to conclude that an intruder lurked in some corner, waiting for me to let my guard down. Why? Because my frame of reference in that setting was based on

- what I heard,
- what I could *not* see,
- what I believed to be happening, and
- what I surmised the only probable cause to be.

We *see* what we *believe* to be happening based on what we *know* in the moment. Such is the power of perspective at play.

SOLO PARENT PRINCIPLE

The story we tell ourselves about what is happening in our lives shapes the worldview we pass on to our children. This is exactly why the proper ongoing perspective is so crucial while parenting solo.

Immediately Jesus made the disciples get into the boat and go on ahead of him to the other side, while he dismissed the crowd. After he had dismissed them, he went up on a mountainside by himself to pray. Later that night, he was there alone, and the boat was already a considerable distance from land, buffeted by the waves because the wind was against it. Shortly before dawn Jesus went out to them, walking on the lake. When the disciples saw him walking on the lake, they were terrified. "It's a ghost," they said, and cried out in fear. But Jesus immediately said to them: "Take courage! It is I. Don't be afraid."

MATTHEW 14:22-27

The only frame of reference the disciples had for someone walking on water in high winds and waves was a ghost. That's the only explanation that made sense to them. That's all they believed was possible, so that is exactly what they saw.

But in both my Barbie story and this Jesus encounter, what was believed to be happening was not even close to the reality. Our individual perspective—formed by past experience coupled with our beliefs—influences how we view situations and circumstances in life.

My perspective started changing in my solo season. My beliefs started changing too. I went from feeling overwhelmed to finding peace, even though the storms of life were very real and the waves were still crashing around me. I chose to believe God was at work even in this strange season and started to look for evidence that He was. When I looked for Him on the waves, I always found Him. Every time. You can too.

Priest and author Henri Nouwen writes, "Make the conscious choice to move the attention of your anxious heart away from the waves and direct it to the One who walks on them and says, 'It's me. Don't be afraid.' . . . Look at him and say, 'Lord, have mercy.' Say it again and again, not anxiously but with confidence that he is very close to you and will put your soul to rest."[1]

If we don't choose to look for God around us, then it is not likely we won't believe He is actually at work. Because our perception becomes our reality. For this reason, we must be deliberate about shaping our perspective in our solo season.

If we're honest, most of us coming out of years of a toxic relationship and the ending of a marriage have a lousy life perspective. Only intentional work in this area will make us healthy, faith-filled, and positive people again.

A pastor friend of mine once shared a perspective that I have never forgotten.

"Robert," he told me, "do you know why winter seasons are so important to farmers? They know that without a good winter, when everything seemingly dies on the surface, the root systems aren't able to build up the energy for a healthy new crop. Without sufficient chilling time, a fruit tree will generate fewer, weaker buds, limiting fruit production from day one. You can't have a good spring without a hearty winter."

That's put-it-on-the-fridge material for us right there: *You can't have a good spring without a hearty winter.*

Now with Barbara in my life, I could actually see a potential *spring,* and it was very obvious that *winter* had made my roots grow stronger and permanently changed my perspective for the better.

4. The Power of Prayer

While listing the four Ps, I intentionally separated *pause* and *prayer.* Understandably, *prayer* could easily be the first choice we make. But for me, praying during this season took on a very different position and posture than at any other time in my life.

As a Christian, especially growing up as a missionary kid, prayer had always been a part of my life. But during this season, I moved from having a daily, formal time of prayer to an ongoing, open line of communication between my Father and me. In a very real way, my religious activities took a back seat to a desperately needed relationship with my heavenly Dad. Of course I would still set aside designated times to bring my requests before Him, but my new prayer mode also involved communicating in real time as life happened.

On my way to pick up the girls from school, I would pray a quick phrase such as, "Father, guide my conversations with my daughters."

Just before I had to appear in court regarding another custody issue, I would whisper, "Father, please give me *Your* words."

As I walked up the stairs to my office, I would say, "Lord, I need Your strength and focus today."

When I would receive a phone call from my ex-wife, I would think, *Father, help me to focus only on what is important and best for the girls.*

Like never before, I knew God was with me every day, everywhere, in all circumstances, and I started living, speaking, and praying from that frame of reference.

This added dimension to my prayer life helped me to feel less alone, and I continually experienced God intersecting with my everyday life. This particularly difficult season of not knowing how to deal with raising girls birthed this new aspect of my relationship with God.

Here is one prayer that I used often:

God,
Grant me eyes to see beyond actions to the need and deficit
*   of the situation.*
Grant me wisdom to not correct what is part of Your process.
Grant me grace that gently leads to Your peace.
Grant me strength to stand against the snare of the adversary.
Grant me love to cover my girls' wounds.
Grand me faith to surrender to Your parenting, accepting
*   the weight of only what You would have me do.*
Grant me peace to still my impatience.
Grant me hope to know You are faithful.
Amen.

If you follow these four principles—Pause, Practices, Perspective, and Prayer—they will lead you to one more important "P."

Possibilities

Whether you are newly divorced or lost your spouse years ago, always remember that God is at work, offering you new possibilities.

Early in my solo season, thinking positively about what might be possible for me was not even on my radar. Survival was my only focus, and it took everything I had just to function day in and day out. But by following these four principles, slowly and methodically, as if I were that well-worn log in the Seine River, I had made a permanent change in my life—not only in the day-to-day challenges, but also in reinforcing the belief that God is not done with me yet and there is actually hope for a better life. Maybe even a life to be shared again, maybe with Barb.

Coincidentally, while I had three girls, she had three boys. Yes, we potentially could be a "Brady Bunch," albeit inverted. Sing the theme song if you want.

The ages of our kids dovetailed perfectly in order—my oldest, then her oldest, then my middle child, then her middle child, then my youngest, and her youngest—ranging at that time between eight and fourteen years old. Both of us had full-time custody of our children. If I hadn't lived it, I would have a hard time believing such a similar match was even possible. (Remember my analogy about finding a train on the same track, already going our speed and then linking up? That analogy was now starting to make sense.)

Yet the thought of potentially merging these two families caused me to take just one step at a time.

After we had dated for a few months, we felt that it was time for us to meet each other's kids and for them to meet each other. When I told my girls about the meeting, they were not super excited about Dad having another love interest apart from them.

The first time the girls met Barb, their attitude was standoffish. They weren't rude, but they weren't exactly warm either. I remember thinking, *I don't think they like the idea of sharing me.* We had become a clan, a very close tribe that, from their point of view, wasn't lacking anything. *So tell us again why we need her, Dad?*

This was, of course, both good *and* bad. I was glad the girls thought our family unit was strong and not in need of anything else besides each other and God. But God knew what we *all* needed next more than any of us did. If God meant for Barb and me to be together, then I would need to stretch my daughters' comfort zones. God doesn't bring His will to us as solo parents and forget His will for the children—it's either His will for us all as a family or it's not—and that also applied to Barb and her sons. I had to discern what God was saying to us and then communicate and navigate well in leading our families to a potentially new destination. But I was already beginning to sense this would not be easy.

10
CARRIED TO THE TABLE

I WAS STANDING AT an emotional crossroads.

The journey with my girls over the previous five years had led us to a place of unity. Together we experienced healing as we worked through many hurts and hurdles; we had overcome so much, which created an incredible bond between us. Even though life after the divorce began as a "desert experience," we had grown comfortable with the "new normal."

But this new journey with Barb—along with her three boys—was now intersecting. There I stood, staring at these two merging lanes, knowing the way my girls felt about sharing me, while also fully aware of how I felt for Barb and she felt for me.

I imagine how the Israelites must have felt after spending all that time in the wilderness as they witnessed God's provision and miraculous interventions time after time. Life in the wilderness had become a new normal. And so, when they reached the border of the Promised Land, fear crept into their minds and hearts again. Another change. Another challenge. The people occupying the land were bigger. How would they be able to take hold of it? On their own, they were outnumbered and weaker.

My girls' attitudes presented an impasse, but surely God hadn't brought us to this point just for everything to fall apart now.

At some point I knew I would have to trust that the same God who had brought me this far knew exactly how to navigate this new challenge. He had proven His faithfulness over and over, and if this was what I believed God wanted, dare I say promised, then that had to be enough.

But the question remained: Was my girls' *immediate* discomfort part of God's plan? It sounded like my decision made sense on paper, but to disrupt what had become our normal was a big decision. How could I be sure this was God's will?

As solo parents, Barb and I agreed it wasn't worth dating just to date. I had no desire to be a bachelor father of three girls who entertained casual relationships. There was no room for that lifestyle. From our very first date, I felt as if I'd found someone who would make a great life partner. The feeling went deeper than chemistry, even though that element was strong from the start.

Say Something

After about a year of dating, Barb and I began discussing marriage. We would speak about it in the beginning in "what-ifs." We wanted the same things in raising our families and life direction, so over time we evolved into "Can we?" And finally, our agreement and resolve ended at "We will."

Two years into the relationship, we were both convinced this was *right*. But we disagreed on one thing—timing.

I had this gut-level feeling that taking our time to merge our two family cultures, personalities, preferences, and also our individual wounds was the right approach. I felt at peace about getting married but not anytime soon. If there was a significant issue Barb and I dealt with, this was it. She is a black-and-white thinker, which is an incredibly valuable perspective compared with my creative, "embrace the gray" approach to life. So for her, once you make the decision to do something, you do it. You commit. And I love that about her. I, on the other hand, hold fast to timing being everything.

To this day, I am not exactly sure why I couldn't feel released from believing we needed to wait a little longer. Did God plan this so I could undo more of the impulsive patterns I exhibited through much of my life, or so Barb would surrender more control of her practical planning and deepen her trust? Or was I simply afraid? I had no idea. I *did* worry that she would grow tired of the waiting and decide to move on. To her credit, although we talked this through often, she rarely complained, never gave me an ultimatum, and was graciously patient.

My reluctance led to three years of dating when we both knew we wanted to be married to each other. But everyone has limits. I didn't know at the time but Barb was starting to consider that our marriage was never going to happen and she would have to be the one to let me go.

The timing of moving on to another marriage is a delicate balancing act. Yet I would encourage you always to err on the side of taking more time. I prayed daily for God to make His timing clear, and honestly, I don't feel He gave me a clear sign. I decided that until I had an overwhelming compulsion to take the next step I would wait. As I tried to be completely dependent to Him, I had removed the God-given sensibilities that He creates within all of us. Sometimes our heavenly Father speaks to us through our own human understanding instead of a miraculous word.

One night I was at home alone watching late-night TV. A duo called A Great Big World, along with Christina Aguilera, was performing their hit song called "Say Something." I was riveted and started crying as I listened to the haunting song's lyrics that mentioned swallowing pride and saying good-bye. And then I heard the key line: "Say something, I'm giving up on you."

I realized this must have been how Barb was feeling— and I was devastated. This song helped me feel the weight of waiting from her perspective. Unbeknownst to me, this same song had resonated deep within her as well, expressing exactly her feelings.

I did wonder if God used this season of waiting to move us *both* to a breaking point. I now felt the desperate ache of not being with Barb as my wife and partner, as an amazing complement to me, as one whom my soul deeply needed on a level I had never experienced before. I know now that she was at a breaking point too and feeling the pain of possibly having to let go of something she believed was right.

I believe with all my heart that timing is a critical part of God's process. It is not our job to understand the timing. It's more about trusting God with the time, and letting Him use the moments to mold us into who we need to be for the purpose or promise He has for us.

For the first time I truly understood what God saw in Adam when He said it is not good for man to be alone. That night I felt the passion, resolve, and peace to ask her to marry me. And I knew beyond any doubt that this was not only the right *thing* to do, but also the right *time*!

SOLO PARENT PRINCIPLE

Being ready to remarry requires a major mind-set shift. Your focus changes from being the parent of your children exclusively to sharing the role of parenting with the person with whom you will become "one."

This decision meant it was time to have a heart-to-heart with my girls, another life-changing conversation. The first one was when I told them their mother was gone; that was the end of the only lifestyle they knew. My marriage to Barb would be another complete change from the almost eight years of having me to themselves.

They had grown accustomed to me dating, to Barb, and to her sons being a part of our lives on weekends, holidays, trips, and vacations together. For the most part, the children got along well, even though they might not have admitted it. But at the end of every outing, Barb and the boys went home, leaving the girls and me to our own house and our own lives.

Just like before, we gathered in my bedroom as I began.

"Girls, you know nothing will ever change my love for you. Nothing can or ever will change us as a family—me being your dad who loves you completely, and you as my daughters who are irreplaceable. Barb and I have been dating for three years now, and I love her and believe she makes my life so much better, and frankly, I believe she makes *our* lives better. So I am planning to ask her to marry me."

Tears started welling up in their eyes, as if I were betraying them and stealing away their last vestige of stability. In complete agreement, they protested, "No, Dad! You can't! Just keep dating! Wait until we are all out of the house! We don't want everything changing and having boys move in!"

I stayed calm and reassured them. "I know there will be a lot of change for us all, but you're going to have to trust me. I believe this is best in the long run. I would never do anything selfishly that would not benefit all of us. I am not asking you to see that now. I am just asking you to trust me."

Then came all the logistical questions: Who changes rooms? Where would they stay? Will they have to have stricter rules since boys are loud and annoying? I assured them everything would be considered and they wouldn't have to change rooms. I also reminded them that girls can be dramatic and annoying too. I promised that although it would be messy for a while, we would get through the adjustment and be better on the other side.

Although this was a difficult conversation, afterward I felt a huge weight off my shoulders. It brought an even stronger resolve that marrying Barb was the right thing, and the *orbiting oddity* I discussed earlier was beginning to make a healthy shift. I also sensed the excitement of beginning a new chapter.

Love—Tailored for You

During my eight-year solo season I had learned several lessons.

- I had failed in key relationships and left damage in my wake.
- I had lived for myself and tried to hold it all together alone.
- I was broken by my own doing.
- God doesn't accept, love, and care for me based on my performance.
- Regardless of my past and even current actions, I am a son of the King.
- I am adored, fought for, and constantly pursued by my Father.
- He loves me beyond what I bring to the relationship.
- His love is fueled by an intense desire to have a relationship with me regardless of my current condition.

The love I have for my girls as their father is the closest thing I can compare to this spiritual dynamic. I would do *anything* for them and, yet, I fully realize that as a sinner I also have a heart of selfishness.

The love I had come to know *and* ultimately accept during this season—two quite different stages in knowledge and acceptance—went beyond anything I had ever experienced up to this point in my life. God's grip on me was relentless, trustworthy, ferocious, and yet tender. His love was true intimacy carved out exclusively for me. My name was on the lips of the God of the universe—I AM—and I know now that when He speaks, telling me everything is under His control, He is caring for me. Despite how circumstances sometimes look, I believe Him. He has proven His faithfulness to me time and again.

As a fearful, worrisome dad of three girls, knowing I would never be a perfect father and now walking into yet another season of disruption, I had to realize my daughters' names were also on the lips of the same powerful God— I AM—who had the same exclusive passion and love for them individually. So often I was consumed by how the dark twists and turns of our family's life were damaging the girls and how I was unable to undo the scars left on them by the divorce and everything surrounding it. But one morning as I was confessing my fears to God, I heard His voice. That quiet, familiar voice heard within my heart said, "Robert, you have come to know how much I love you. Haven't you come to know how I take care of you, how I give grace, how I provide and protect, how I see you right where you are, with all the regrets, bumps, and bruises of a complex life, how My love is tailored for you?"

I could only whisper, "Yes, Father," as He continued.

"Do you think I love Zoe, Skyler, and Zara any less? With the same relentless and tender love I authored their lives, I see right where they are, I know them intimately, and I can be trusted with their hearts and lives. Just as I gave you grace to find your way to Me, I give them grace. But make no mistake; they are never out of My reach. They are precious to Me. You aren't and shouldn't be in control of their destiny. Just do your best to pursue their hearts and leave the rest to Me."

What humbling words. Ones I desperately needed.

As I looked ahead to the work of blending a family, I was considering myself solely responsible for the welfare of my girls. God often uses disruptions to make us lean into Him more. I knew He used the obstacles and heartache as a way of shaping us, but I needed to be reminded. He used my growing up in Africa, being torn from one culture to another, my parents' divorce, and so many other things in my childhood to mold me into the person I had become. He was now continuing to use the experiences of living in a home of active addiction, instability, and a divorce to shape my girls. As my mentor, Clive Calder, used to say, "It's not about how you start, but how you end."

What, then, shall we say in response to these things? If God is for us, who can be against us? He who did not spare his own Son, but gave him up for us all—how will he not also, along with him, graciously give us all things? Who will bring any charge against those whom God has chosen? It is God who justifies. Who then is the one who condemns? No one. Christ Jesus who died—more than that, who was raised to life—is at the right side of God and is also interceding for us. Who shall separate us from the love of Christ? Shall trouble or hardship or persecution or famine or nakedness or danger or sword? . . . No, in all these things we are more than conquerors through him who loved us. For I am convinced that neither death nor life, neither angels nor demons, neither the present nor the future, nor any powers, neither height nor depth, nor anything else in all creation, will be able to separate us from the love of God that is in Christ Jesus our Lord.

ROMANS 8:31-35, 37-39

A Perfect Match

Now, with all this confirmation, there was still one detail left: Barb needed to say *yes*.

I wanted to ask her while we were alone and in a meaningful setting, but time after time when I planned "the moment," something would happen. With six kids, that's life, right? But one evening in February, she met me at my house for our weekly date night while the girls were away. Finally, we were actually alone. So in the front entryway of my house, I got down on one knee with a diamond ring, and said, "I'm sorry this isn't a more romantic setting, but I can't wait any longer. Will you marry me?"

She said, "Yes," and my heart felt so full!

That night at dinner, we began to strategize. Because we planned to move her family into my house and her boys had to change schools, we set the date for as soon as we felt possible—four months later on June 7, after school let out for the summer. The wedding would be outside my house, as we symbolically reclaimed the home on the hill as ours, making all things new.

It would be a small, simple wedding overlooking a stream at the bottom of our tree-lined hill at 7:00 p.m., just as the sun would be setting behind the trees. The reception would be inside the house. My friend, Father Thomas, who had been a significant source of encouragement and strength throughout my solo season, would officiate. Tiffany Lee, better known as the Christian artist Plumb, whom I had signed and developed, would sing. God was bringing everything together even in our compressed time frame.

February to June passed quickly, and our wedding day brought a beautiful morning. I had heard there might be some showers in the afternoon, but the forecast promised a nice, cool evening. Chairs and flowers were delivered. The caterer was prepping food. The decor around the house was coming together. A natural arrangement of branches was set up as the altar.

Everything was ready by 4:00 p.m. so I sat down for the first time all day and started gathering a playlist of songs for the reception. About 4:30 I received this text from Jeff, a record-producer friend and self-proclaimed weather nerd who would be the DJ at the reception:

"Hey man, have you seen the forecast? I hate to be

the one to tell you this, but serious storms are building
to the west of us. National Weather Service just issued
a major thunderstorm warning for our county. I just
looked at the radar. Looks like it's headed directly for
Franklin."

Just as Jeff described, there was a huge front headed
straight for us with heavy rain, lightning, and strong winds,
hitting between 5:00 and 9:00 p.m. I had to tell Barb, so I
started praying as earnestly as I could that the storm would
pass just before the ceremony, and lead to a beautiful, clear
sunset, just as we had imagined.

After this long road, all the heartache, all the struggles,
surely God would not allow a storm to ruin this long-
awaited moment.

Strength in the Storm

At 6:00 p.m. light rain fell, and my stepdad and Barb's
father started covering the chairs with tarps and carrying
the sound system inside.

By 6:15, the rain was heavier and the sky darker, and as
guests began to arrive the winds picked up and lightning
flashed in the distance. We decided we had no choice but
to move the wedding inside. No sunset. No cool summer
breeze. I felt deflated. Barb did too. But we would make
the best of it, exactly as we had always done during our
years of being solo parents.

The guests were packed in, the violinist began playing, and Barbara looked gorgeous as she walked down
the stairs and into the entryway. When my wife-to-be

rounded the corner and came into view, the tears started coming. By nature, I am a crier. Watching her walk toward me on her father's arm, surrounded by our fractured families and so many dear friends who had walked with us, had more beauty and significance than if we had been standing outside under the trees facing a stunning summer sunset.

In that surreal moment, I realized we were standing at the *very place* where I had faced an open door and discovered the vacant master bedroom and my ex-wife's departure eight years before.

Outside, the rain poured, the winds blew violently, and lightning flashed in the darkened sky. I realized this was exactly where God wanted us to be. While the world raged around us, we were safe in His care and grace. Now laying aside the past that had left us broken, we were standing at the threshold of a new beginning.

Father Thomas offered profoundly appropriate words:

"As we look at this couple, let's remember no one would have ever wished or planned on being in this situation. Some still may not be happy about it, and that's okay because God is in the business of redeeming situations. There will always be circumstances that we don't wish for, plan on, or want, but turning those situations into something beautiful is what He has always been about and what He will always be about."

At that point for me, everything became crystal clear. We didn't wish or plan on our marriages ending. Some of our kids may have not wanted this new beginning. We certainly didn't want the storm that was surrounding us. But in the midst of it all, we could trust that God was restoring, reviving, reminding, and redeeming everything that was broken and turning it into something even better. That's what He does.

The whole evening was a living example of the contrast between our best-laid plans and the greater desires our heavenly Father has for our good. The death of a dream can make way for His greater purpose.

You would think all the surprises we encountered were enough for one evening. But halfway through the reception, I received a call.

"Robert?"

"Yes," I answered.

"I am sorry I have to tell you this, but Barbara's neighbor just called me because she couldn't reach her. The storm hit hard here and knocked a massive tree down in her backyard. In fact, it hit with such force that it ripped the gas line out of the house. I don't know how extensive the damage is, but police have it roped off, and there is a backhoe and utility workers feverishly working around her house. They had to officially lock down her neighborhood and shut down the entire gas grid."

After giving Barb the news, I was amazed at how my new wife handled this tragedy. Obviously, she was upset and worried because Tux, her dog, was still in the house. But knowing it was out of her control and nothing could be done because we weren't even allowed to be in the area, she chose to hope and pray for the best and started to dance again. She made the choice to enjoy what was right in front of us. She chose to focus on her new perspective.

By the time we were cleared to enter her house around midnight, we could still smell gas. But in the darkness, we heard Tux. Other than being frightened, he was fine. The house, however, was destroyed. So on our wedding night, with only headlamps and flashlights, we picked our way through the soaked remains of her home gathering valuables. If any of the twelve family members staying with Barb for the wedding had been in the house when that tree came down, I have no doubt the tragedy would have taken lives. Miraculously, anything significant and valuable to Barb had been spared.

One of Barb's concerns about adjusting to married life was leaving the house she and the boys had lived in for so many years. Their memories, good and bad, were tied to that house. Would she be able to walk away from the home that had come to symbolize family to her and the boys?

Sometimes when God opens a door, He closes another. I am not saying God destroyed her house, but I will say that it wasn't lost on Barb that it is easier to walk away from a house that was devastated than one full of pristine memories. I do know this: I believe that even the destruction served a greater purpose in many ways, as hard as it was for us to have to spend our wedding night crawling around in the remains of her house.

What mattered now was that we were married. Our families were safe. The home in which we would all live was perfectly intact. What the enemy intended for evil, God had redeemed for good (Genesis 50:20).

The Crippled and the King

The last artist I had signed to my label was a young man named Leeland Mooring. We called his band Leeland. When I met him, he was only fourteen years old, but his wisdom and insight were far beyond his years. He reminded me of what King David must have been like in his youth, speaking with such conviction about things he believed God had shown him. At his age, this certainly didn't come from life experiences. You hear the buzzword of "anointed" in Christian circles, but in Leeland's case, I believe it was the only explanation.

A song he wrote with Marc Byrd and Steve Hindalong was called "Carried to the Table."

Wounded and forsaken
I was shattered by the fall
Broken and forgotten
Feeling lost and all alone
Summoned by the King
Into the Master's courts
Lifted by the Savior
And cradled in His arms

I was carried to the table
Seated where I don't belong
Carried to the table
Swept away by His love
And I don't see my brokenness anymore
When I'm seated at the table of the Lord

I'm carried to the table
The table of the Lord

Fighting thoughts of fear
And wondering why He called my name
Am I good enough to share this cup
This world has left me lame
Even in my weakness
The Savior called my name
In His holy presence
I'm healed and unashamed

You carried me, my God
You carried me[1]

I sat down with him to discuss the meaning of his lyrics. When I heard this teenager explain his perspective, it became one of those never-forget, life-altering encounters.

He said the song was based on 2 Samuel 9, written from the point of view of a crippled man named Mephibosheth who had nothing. This man was from the family of King Saul, and in that day, the new king would often kill the former king's remaining family so no challenge to the throne could remain. So when David ordered his men to bring Mephibosheth to his court, Mephibosheth believed he would be executed. Instead, David welcomed him and gave him a permanent seat at the king's table.

Now that story of forgiveness, restoration, compassion, and humility is touching, but here's where Leeland's explanation really got me. Even though Mephibosheth was invited to the king's table, he couldn't walk. He had to be carried. Not only was he not worthy to be at the table, but in his condition he couldn't even come to the table without humbling himself even further and accepting help.

Mephibosheth was just like me.

After the divorce, I came to believe that God could make me whole. Yet even though I had been invited to the King's table in those early solo parent days, I didn't know how to get there.

Just like the crippled Mephibosheth, I had to be carried too. I was carried by the love of my community, the healing of time, the tangible restoration that took place in my home. Inch by inch, moment by moment, day by day, I was carried to the table by Jesus Christ, the King of kings, and the people of His Kingdom.

Leeland concluded with this knockout punch of truth: "When a crippled beggar is seated at the table, you no longer can see he is a cripple. He looks the same and is at the same level as the rest of the guests, even the same as the king. So to be seated at the table is not only an honor, but a way of removing the handicap from view, a way to be seen as equal and whole."

That is how God sees us. That is what God offers us. That is what God will do for us—for you.

None Other Has Ever Known

I am truly honored that you have allowed me to share my journey with you. If I were able to sit across from you right now, look you in the eye, and wrap up our time together,

I would tell you these final thoughts and ask you to prayerfully consider them.

Please know that I am no one special. Just because my journey has been chronicled in this book makes it no greater than the one you are on right now. We share a similar path, and God has us both right where He wants us. We would never have chosen to be solo parents. But I promise God knows all about every conflicting feeling, every overwhelming moment, every broken piece of every dream, every empty space that used to be filled, every ache in the deepest part of you, every secret, and every need. He knows.

Jesus is with you, and you are enough just as you are, broken and dependent. In this broken place, God can build something beautiful, something far beyond what you can do alone, and far beyond what a mate can do. Remember, God is already restoring you.

My hope is that you take the time to know how loved you are, right here and now, just as you are. Most importantly, I hope you come to see that there is a sacred event happening in your life. You are being carried to a holy place. Solo is the place where God met me. Solo is where He can meet you, too.

Back in 1912, in his cold, dreary, and leaky basement with no windows, C. Austin Miles wrote these words:

> *I come to the Garden alone,*
> *While the dew is still on the roses,*
> *And the voice I hear, falling on my ear,*
> *The Son of God discloses.*
> *And He walks with me, and He talks with me,*

And He tells me I am His own,
And the joy we share as we tarry there,
None other has ever known.

I close my eyes, picturing a quiet garden, hidden from the world. There is a stone bench surrounded by the lush, cool, quiet of trees and bushes with a babbling brook and birds chirping. I come and sit and wait. I pay attention to the stillness. Here I find peace. And if I wait long enough, I hear the rustling of someone quietly moving toward me. It is Jesus. He sits down by me. I start to cry. I let go. I let the Lord take my burdens, my regrets, my shame, and my pain. I let Him see how broken I am. I hear His voice reassuring me. Like "none other has ever known" when "I come to the Garden alone."

I am here to tell you, this place is real. Jesus actually shows up if we wait quietly for Him in this still space. My prayer is that you, too, look for and come to find God in this garden, that you come to find this place of true wholeness. And I pray that you believe, like I believe, that your journey through this valley is for a purpose, that it will lead to a transformational encounter with the God of the universe who turns our ashes into something far beyond anything we can ask or imagine.

Your journey won't look exactly like mine; it will be different. Yet it will be the same in this way: If you allow Jesus to do so, He will author a path that leaves you and your children better off than you were before, better than where you are now, and even better than you can fathom in your future.

Jesus carries you to His table, forever.

ACKNOWLEDGMENTS

NEVER IN MY WILDEST imagination would I have dreamed that one day I'd have a story to tell and the honor of being an author. A story is only as valuable as the characters in it; some are mentioned in this book by name, other names have been changed, and some are not mentioned but have played an equally important role in bringing my story, and this book, to life. I am eternally grateful for each and every one.

To Brad Schmitt—I never would have started this process if not for you spending countless hours with me writing out my story and believing I had one to tell. You inspire me.

To Brian Mitchell, my agent and friend for more than two decades—Thanks for not only giving everything you have to get this book out, but also for the incredible support you were as a friend and godfather to my girls during my solo season. And to your wife, Kim Mitchell, my podcast cohost—thanks for jumping in with both feet. And thanks to Bill Reeves and the entire WTA agency for believing.

To Robert Noland—I literally would not have been able to get this done without your expertise and godly wisdom. But more than that, I cherish our friendship!

To my family—I love you all. Zoe, Skyler, and Zara: As I said in my dedication, there is nothing on this earth that I treasure more than being your dad. Each one of you is remarkable in your own way, and I am so proud of the heart God has placed in each of you. Never ever think it's too late or you are too far gone for God to work in your life in ways that are beyond what you think is possible (my transformation started in my forties). He is faithful! Mom, I dedicated this book to your memory because had it not been for our daily phone calls during my solo season I am not sure I would have ended up here on the other side as resolved in my assurance of my Father's love and care for me. Dad and Marie: Thanks for being so steadfast and consistent. Jim: I am so proud of you for making your own life changes to be a great solo dad to Bela. Sandy: You loved my mom well until her dying day, and in doing that, you loved me well. To my late mother-in-law Sharon (Grams): We are forever indebted to you for giving your everything for the sake of your granddaughters and me. Jace, Kyler, and Brennan Avellino: You guys are awesome, and I am so grateful I get to share this life with you and be your stepdad. Ralph, Sue, Ryan, and Gavyn Domato, and Fred, Pam, Maddie, and Ellie Ferris: Thanks for welcoming the girls and me as family from day one. To all the Carlsons: Thanks for sticking with and loving the girls and me even after the "in-law" title left. You never stopped treating us like family.

To my iShine family—Tom Johnson, who has sacrificed

and taught me so much about leadership and the importance of 'walking with a limp.' To my comrade Brad Mathias and family, for demonstrating authentic parenting and a passionate pursuit of the heart of our kids. Alexis, you have been like family since I met you when you were twelve. I am so proud and grateful for you. Mimi, you have been like a mom to me and a grandma to the girls. We love you.

To my unstoppable friends who gave so much of themselves in my solo season—Troy and Stacy Collins and family, Nate Larkin, Fr. Thomas Mackenzie, Jeromy Deibler, Liz Thurman, and Heidi Schlieckau.

To my amazing neighbors at the Ridge—Our little community is so rare and was, and is, so valuable to our family.

To Jordyn Thomas and Nina Woodard—There is no way to thank you enough for the countless ways you stepped up, filled the gap, and made so many amazing memories with the girls and me.

To Darren and Brandy Whitehead and everyone at Church of the City, Franklin—For believing and providing a perfect platform to launch Solo Parent Society life groups. Mike Smith and David Smallbone—Your friendship and encouragement opened the doors that laid a foundation for launching the groups. To the Solo Parent Society launch team—Amber, Missy, Sarah, Paige, Brian, and Dave. You all are amazing! To the Solo Parent Society life group members who contributed to the book—Brian, Kevin, Kendra, Joye, Carol, and Kristen. Your insights were invaluable. To the Solo Parent Society board—Dave Farmer, Brent Gray, and Robert Noland. I am grateful for your leadership and passion.

To Sissy Goff and Daystar counseling ministries—
Thank you for the care you have given our family.

To Troy Duhon and family—Thanks for believing and
so passionately encouraging and pushing me to pursue
my calling.

To my Essential Records and Provident Label Group
family—I loved what we were able to do together. The artists I had the honor of working with—Jars of Clay, Third
Day, Caedmons Call, Casting Crowns, Michael W. Smith,
Bebo Norman, Plumb, Joy Williams, Leeland, Andrew
Peterson, and so many more. Thanks for allowing me to
get into your creative space. I am proud of what we had
the opportunity to do together.

Thanks to the team at Focus on the Family—Jim Daly,
Bob DeMoss, Larry Weeden, Julie Holmquist, and
Dante Miro.

To my ex-wife—If you read this, I pray you don't get
the impression that I think this tragedy was all your fault.
It wasn't. My prayer is that maybe through hearing about
my journey through the mess we made, you can find hope
and healing too. Thank you for bringing three of the most
amazing souls to life.

Lastly, but arguably most importantly, thanks to my wife,
Barbara Beeson, for being my anchor. God knew exactly
what He was doing when He allowed our solo parent paths
to cross. I am blessed every day that I get to call you my wife
and best friend, and I look forward to building something
amazing together as a testimony of God's faithfulness.

As you can see, I am blessed.

NOTES

CHAPTER 2: VOICE OF TRUTH

1. Mark Hall, Steven Curtis Chapman, "Voice of Truth," Copyright © 2003 My Refuge Music (BMI) Sparrow Song (BMI) (adm. at CapitolCMGPublishing .com) / Be Essential Songs (BMI) / Peach Hill Songs (BMI). All rights reserved. Used by permission.
2. Albert Barnes, "Barnes' Notes on the Bible," 1834, *Bible Hub*, accessed July 25, 2017, http://biblehub.com/commentaries/exodus/3-14.htm.

CHAPTER 5: DECIDING TO DANCE

1. Sissy Goff, interview by Robert Besson, "The Importance of Boundaries," Solo Parent Society podcast, February 20, 2017, https://itunes.apple.com /us/podcast/solo-parent-society/id1210812663.
2. *Merriam-Webster*, http://www.merriamwebster.com/dictionary/charity.
3. John Chirban, interview by Robert Beeson and Kimberley Mitchell, "Putting Kids in the Middle," Solo Parent Society podcast, March 29, 2017, https:// soundcloud.com/soloparentsociety/ep6-dr-john-chirban-p2.

CHAPTER 6: MY ONE SAFE PLACE

1. Sara Lazar, "How Meditation Can Shape Our Brains," YouTube video, TEDxCambridge 2011, posted January 23, 2012, https://www.youtube .com/watch?v=m8rRzTtP7Tc.
2. *The Oxford Dictionary*, http:en.oxforddictionaries.com/difinition /redemption.
3. *The Oxford Dictionary*, http:en.oxforddictionaries.com/difinition /restoration.

CHAPTER 7: A FIRM PLACE TO STAND
1. Chirban, "Putting Kids in the Middle."
2. George Barna, email message to author, July 8, 2017.
3. "Research Shows That Spiritual Maturity Process Should Start at a Young Age," Barna Group, November 17, 2003, https://www.barna.com/research/research-shows-that-spiritual-maturity-process-should-start-at-a-young-age/.
4. "Evangelism Is Most Effective Among Kids," Barna Group, October 11, 2004, https://www.barna.com/research/evangelism-is-most-effective-among-kids/.
5. Max Lucado, *You'll Get Through This: Hope and Help for Your Turbulent Times* (Nashville, TN: Thomas Nelson, 2015), 70.

CHAPTER 9: LIKE A CITY ON A HILL
1. Henri Nouwen, *Inner Voice of Love: A Journey Through Anguish to Freedom* (New York: Random House, 2010), 98.

CHAPTER 10: CARRIED TO THE TABLE
1. Leeland Mooring, Marc Byrd, and Steve Hindalong, "Carried to the Table," Copyright © 2006 Meaux Mercy (BMI), Meaux Hits (ASCAP), Blue Raft Music (BMI), Colorwheel Songs (ASCAP) (adm. at CapitolCMGPublishing.com). All rights reserved. Used by permission.